OUR DOGS

OUR DOGS

A Century of Images and Words From the AKC GAZETTE

American Kennel Club

Ballantine Books
New York

A Ballantine Book
Published by The Random House Publishing Group

Copyright © 2003 by the AKC Gazette

All rights reserved under International and Pan-American Copyright Conventions. Published in the United States by The Random House Publishing Group, a division of Random House, Inc., New York, and simultaneously in Canada by Random House of Canada Limited, Toronto.

Ballantine and colophon are registered trademarks of Random House, Inc.

www.ballantinebooks.com

Book design by C. Linda Dingler

The Library of Congress Cataloging-in-Publication Data is available from the publisher.

ISBN 0-345-46629-2

Manufactured in the United States of America

First Edition: November 2003

10 9 8 7 6 5 4 3 2 1

Acknowledgments

AKC Publications staff contributing their efforts in compiling this book included George Berger, Russell Bianca, Tanya Bielski-Braham, Bud Boccone, Rocco Buchicchio, Ginny Gonzalez, Tilly Grassa, Kathryn Klanderman, Meghan Lyons, Erika Mansourian, Bianca Moscatelli, Arliss Paddock, Melanie Palishen, Rosemarie Silver, Alice Suriani, Bronwyn Taggart, Jacqueline Tomkovich, John Woods, and intern Laura Hendrick.

AKC librarian Barbara Kolk and AKC archivist Geraldine Hayes also provided valued assistance.

Contents

Foreword

by Jane Smiley

I come from a dog family. People in our clan just feel a little wrong if there isn't a dog in the house. When we visit other families that are of the non-dog variety, we secretly wonder how they can stand the quiet—all right, let's be honest—the loneliness and impersonality of a dogless home. No hair on the couch. No dog toys lying around. No barking. No surprises, pleasant or unpleasant. Everything so neat. This does not mean that we agree on breeds. I have been a party to several thin-lipped, exasperated-but-civil family disputes about Labs versus Goldens, Jack Russells versus Fox Terriers. I've never seen anyone converted. My sister and brother stick with Labs. I stick with a mixed population of Great Danes and Jack Russells. My cousins hold out for hunting breeds. That's okay. Someday there will be a big family reunion and all the dogs will come and the Great Danes and Jack Russells will prevail.

People who marry into our family get dogs as part of the package, no matter how resolutely antidog they were before. It's a moral category, actually. If you can't come to love a dog, what sort of person are you? Of course, we keep this thought to ourselves, out of politeness. I personally have converted an antidog man. When he laughs in delight at how the female Jack Russell is smart enough to go up on the roof of the house to find her toys and athletic enough to jump onto the kitchen counters, I smile with extra joy at the fact that his life is so much more lively now that he is a pro-dog man.

In my opinion, three dogs is just the right number. One dog—too focused on the humans. Two dogs—too stable in their relation to one another. Four dogs, five dogs, six dogs—too easy to get lost in the shuffle. Three dogs always have something to do, even if that is only jockeying for position among themselves. Three dogs are never bored. If they get on the humans' nerves, they can always go outside and get on one another's nerves, and pretty soon the humans are looking out the window, laughing at their interactions. On the other hand, three dogs is never too many. One dog out of three is always trying to sleep.

In the course of my life, training theories have changed. The dogs of my youth never saw a crate, or a "lure," or a clicker, or an Invisible Fence. They explored the countryside. They were spanked and ordered about; they were put outside and once in a while the dog-catcher brought one back. They got to be pretty good dogs anyway. Now I take my puppy to dog training class and I marvel at his progress. More than that, I marvel at all my trainer knows about dogs. There has been an explosion in the past twenty-five years in studies of dog behavior and wolf behavior, studies of the learning patterns of dogs, studies of the life cycles and biology and health of dogs. All of this fascinates me, but the fact remains that training theories come and go; it is love and attention that make a good dog.

And so, here is a book for pro-dog men, and women, and children. Here are dogs of all breeds and many eras, pictured in photographs and depicted in words. Some of the once-popular breeds look odd now, and some of the ways people used to think of dogs seem strange. But here is a treasury of dogs. True, they make no noise, they leave no hair on the couch and no toys on the floor, but like all dogs, they are full of surprises and of *life*.

Jane Smiley is the author of ten novels, the mother of three children, and the owner of twelve horses and three dogs. She received the Pulitzer Prize in 1992 for her novel A Thousand Acres.

Introduction

by George Berger

Just next to the front desk of the magnificent American Kennel Club Library in New York is an approximately 8-by-9-foot section of shelves that houses bound volumes of every published issue of the magazine now known as the AKC GAZETTE. On the very top shelf, first book on the left, is the edition catalogued as Volume 1, Number 1. It is dated January 1889. Nearly 1,400 monthly editions later, the AKC GAZETTE today lays easy claim to being the oldest continuously published sporting magazine in the country, and the oldest dog magazine in the world.

The AKC itself was founded in September 1884, in Philadelphia, by a group of thirteen serious-minded gentlemen whose ambition was to ensure the well-being and healthy future of their abiding passion, the sport of purebred dogs. There was substantial progress during the club's first few years, but nothing was as significant as the 1888 election of its fourth president: Harvard-educated, socially established, wildly wealthy, thirty-five-year-old August Belmont Jr. Belmont held the office until 1915; in so doing, and with a dazzling vision of prosperity and excellence for the AKC, he established both stability and direction that had been sorely needed.

Practically from the start of his incumbency, Belmont campaigned for an AKC magazine. Such a publication, he believed, would be a useful tool in helping to achieve his greater objectives: to increase the AKC's growth and influence. Those who opposed the idea of a magazine argued that the costs could destroy the club's already tenuous financial position. But when Belmont pledged to personally underwrite any losses up to $5,000 per year, all objections faded. So, after only months as president, August Belmont Jr. realized one of many dreams, the launch of THE AMERICAN KENNEL GAZETTE. (Incidentally, not a cent of the guaranteed money ever had to be used. Belmont guided the magazine into nearly instantaneous financial success.)

The first issue included the following very earnest statement, directed to member clubs:

The American Kennel Club having adopted the plan of publishing a Gazette, in pursuance of your wishes in the matter, the officers have begun this, its first publication, with the new year, 1889, and they will endeavor, as much as lies in their power, to meet what they feel the Kennel World requires in the shape of an official organ; taking as their guide the expressions of opinion on the subject from breeders and exhibitors, both in the past and since the adoption of the plan of publishing this Gazette.

It is proposed to afford the Kennel Club and its individual members an official medium for the publication of all proceedings and announcements bearing upon any subject embraced by the interests of the Kennel World, and to keep and publish a complete and official record of all that transpires during the year, either in connection with shows, field trials or matters affecting the breeding, kennel, or field management of any known breed of dog.

So it began, and so it has continued (with perhaps just a little more good humor!), the GAZETTE reporting and analyzing an endless variety of subjects "embraced by the interests of the Kennel World" throughout this thrilling, tumultuous, amazing century.

Of course, the interests of the kennel world—people whose lives are touched and influenced by dogs—in most ways parallel the interests of people everywhere. We have all seen too much of the agony and sorrow of war, natural disasters, terrorism, and crime. But we've survived on the strength of valor, faith, resolve, and compassion. And that has been the approach of GAZETTE editors throughout the years: We've reported on the bravery and intelligence of the dogs on active duty during the World Wars; we've described the important work of bomb- and drug-sniffing dogs; we've paid tribute to the search-and-rescue dogs that have saved thousands of human lives.

The idea for this book came nearly three years ago. We had just completed work on one of our special issues of the magazine, and it occurred to us that the material in that edition should be preserved—like so much that had come before it—in a different medium, in a book. Several months passed as we refined the idea. The book would be a twin showcase for important writing and important photography—intentionally independent of each other, married only to the section theme in which they would appear. We would use pictures and stories from the very beginning of the magazine to the most current issue.

The selection process was, frankly, tedious; there was just such a wealth of material to choose from, so relatively little that we could include, so much that was painful to leave out. Our art department staff reviewed some 60,000 photographs; 130 made it into the book.

In some ways even more daunting was the challenge for the editors. All 114 years of GAZETTEs were divided among six of us into fourteen- to twenty-year blocks. We read every word of those issues, looking for stories—whole pieces, long and short excerpts—that would be just right for *Our Dogs.*

In choosing both the text and photography, we held ourselves to the following five criteria; everything had to have at least one of these characteristics:

It had to be beautiful;

It had to represent the era in which it was published;

It had to make a statement about the unique personality of dogs;

It had to be a celebration of dogs' talents;

It had to convey the extraordinary devotion that exists within the human-canine bond.

Considering the massive amount of outstanding material available to us, it is clear that we could easily have a volume two, three, and even four of this book!

The American Kennel Club is a *registry* for purebred dogs. It is widely known as a sanctioning organization for conformation events—the world of "show dogs." But the AKC has expanded its activities and broadened its reach to include all dog-related pursuits. Just as important, the AKC has recognized the emotions of the human relationship with dogs. One highly respected AKC judge said to me not long ago, "The show ring is a really magnificent place, when you stop to think about it. So is the trialing field, so is the tracking course. All of those venues can be full of thrills. But if you ask anyone who is a *real* dog person, through and through, they'll tell you it's not about ribbons and rewards and scores. It's about a basic love, a love of the dog." And that, in the end, is what the GAZETTE, and now *Our Dogs,* are about, too.

In these 114 years, seventeen men and women have steered the GAZETTE on its journalistic course. I am inordinately proud and grateful to be the most recent of them.

George Berger is publisher
of AKC magazines.

OUR DOGS

THE SPECIAL WORLD OF DOGS

Interesting that a word meant for people—personality—fits dogs perfectly.

PHOEBE J. BOOTH

Once again, I sit on the edge of the whelping box eagerly awaiting the new arrivals. How many boys? How many girls? What colors will they be? Will Carrie be a good mother? I am curious, I am excited, I am soothing Carrie—who has no idea that she is about to embark on the most important event in her life. I say to myself that this is indeed what it's all about.

The puppies arrive, one by one, round, and pink, and blind, and helpless, and immediately Carrie nominates herself as Mother of the Year. I have played this scene so many times over the past 30 years, but for Carrie it is her first starring role, and yet, within minutes, she is older, and wiser, and far more capable than I. Yet again, I marvel at the miracle that nature has wrought, and I admire the perfection of each tiny little body. But most of all, I know that now their future is in my hands, and I am sobered by the responsibility and commitment that I feel.

Four weeks later I am sitting on my kitchen floor, which doubles as a puppy room, and I am getting my hair chewed, and my nose bitten, and my face licked, and my shoelaces untied. I am soothing the bumps of the tumbling and tripping puppies, and I'm the referee of the Baby Whippet Wars. Their little legs carry them farther and faster each day, and their individual personalities

Afghan Hound

Golden Retrievers

blossom. Their minds develop just as their bodies grow. Carrie is still an amazingly caring, compassionate, and capable mom, but she is now content to let me handle more of the mundane and boring nursery chores.

Soon the phone will be ringing, and interviews will be given, and families will visit, and each individual spirit will grace the lives of people who, although they may be strangers now, I hope will become my friends through the common bond we will share throughout each little canine life.

For me, this is what it means to be a breeder. Competitions and awards may serve as a means by which we measure our breed-improvement goals, but we should never lose sight of the fact that in those efforts we are creating lives—living, breathing, thinking, feeling, innocent lives who deserve the best that we can offer them. The little pet puppy with the light eyes or the prick ears is just as important as the flyer whose future in the

Opposite: Polish Lowland Sheepdog

4

show ring is bright. The slowest puppy who is reticent to chase the lure deserves as much love and care as the fastest and most athletic.

Being a good breeder means taking complete and total responsibility for every life we've created. It is about finding responsible owners who truly deserve these wonderful creatures, and who take their commitment to them as seriously as we do.

Ribbons fade, records are forgotten, and careers are short. All of those things are meaningless when compared to the character of these special animals whose lives we have engendered. What endures is the loyalty, and love, and uncompromising devotion they give us so freely. We owe each of them the same in equal measure, for their entire lives.

—*November 2002, "What Is a Breeder?"*

West Highland White Terrier

Bulldogs

JERI HOLLOWAY

Dachshunds

He had been picked up that afternoon. Someone called animal control to come get the stray who was hanging around the residential neighborhood. An Irish Setter, he may have been a victim of breed popularity: Fame and glory, followed by overproduction, diminishing popularity, and neglect.

Now at the Louisiana shelter he stood in a cage, waiting. Perhaps four or five years old, he wore no collar. He had some broken teeth, scarred front legs, skin torn away, and deep gashes. It was easy to count his ribs; meals must have been few and far between.

He stood patiently while two people took pictures to record his injured body and malnourished frame. He barely moved and never tried to sit down.

A bright blue lead was placed around his neck, and he was led slowly down a concrete walk to the back door. It was time. The metal basket from the euthanasia room was rolled over to the dog. He was lifted into the basket, his head held high, the eyes gentle and trusting. The basket was rolled into the machine, the door closed and sealed, the buttons pressed.

—*August 1989, "Shelter Life"*

ANNE ELIZABETH BLOCHIN

One of the best things about a small kennel is its social life. Our kennels have always been small, and I hope they will always be so, for personal contact with every individual has given me an insight into the play-life, the personal outlook, and even the business preoccupations of dogs, which becomes more amazing every year. To see the utterly divergent characteristics of litter sisters, for instance, passed down through generations; to find a puppy singing the same heartbreaking tenor as his long-lost grandsire; to witness the complicated game rules worked out in unsupervised canine sport—these and many other observations have been my savor of salt in the mere everyday routine of terrier-raising.

—*July 1932, "Their Infinite Variety"*

ARTHUR FREDERICK JONES

Wisdom is little more than an egotistical fetish of the human race. Man guards this self-termed sagacity with steadfastness which often borders on conceit—yet, man does not really know the meaning of the term wisdom unless he has studied various forms of animal life. And once having learned something of the peculiar depths of the animal brain, he is not so prone to flaunt his own

Irish Setter, 1942

*Miniature Pinscher,
circa 1940*

intelligence, for pure animal wisdom needs no touting heraldry.

This is particularly true in the case of dogs. Sometimes they do such inexplicable things that we are forced to shake our heads and wonder. It is impossible for mere man to explain these actions, for there is the rebel brain which, countless thousands of years ago, chose to forsake Divine reasoning and establish its own standards.

The dog allows his thoughts to be guided by an omnipotence which sees everything, knows all, and can direct its actions in a sensibly correct direction. Such is true of all dogs, although enthusiasts of some breeds, sometimes, claim to discover advantages possessed by no others.

—*December 1925, "Sluggish Bulldogs Are in Fiction"*

Mastiff

ROBERT OLMSTEAD

On Friday, November 22, 1963, at approximately 12:30 P.M., President John F. Kennedy was struck by two rifle bullets while riding in an open limousine through downtown Dallas. The news swept my elementary school like a swift, cruel hand. The importance of this event could not be avoided. I remember it was a dreary day and how my teacher cried, and because I was seven that was more strange to me than the murder of a president. After all, I had learned that the same happened to Abraham Lincoln and that made him an American god, a being whose life transcended death and though dead, forever now remains joyfully alive.

That afternoon I stepped through the bus doors

10

Siberian Husky

to hike the long dirt road where my mother and father had built their house on land gifted them by my grandfather. Waiting for me at the foot of the hill was a big, rangy German Shepherd Dog named Bullet who was in the habit of loping down that hill and ushering me home.

I must have said, "Bullet, they shot President Kennedy," and in Bullet's face was the ever-present look of concern and the appearance of comprehension. I spoke to that dog all the time. I told it thoughts and dreams I would tell to no one else, and I think this is how dogs first seduce us. Their faces are masterful receptors of our projected care, deepest emotions, and most profound wisdom. They are the rare good listeners in a world of talkers. For 15,000 years they have flattered us with their attention and intrigued us with their separateness. I think dogs are our first invention and if not our first, then perhaps our finest.

Golden Retrievers, 1947

I half-think I was raised by German Shepherds. In my child life there were always these great, lumbering, maternal, wolfish animals. They were the smiling, brown-eyed, black and tan dogs who slept in the pine kitchen on a braided rug at the front door. When I was a tiny boy set out to play, they stood between me and the road, nudging my wandering body from the stone wall at the edge of the lawn or the barbed-wire fence beyond which the cattle grazed. I know this because one day when I was older I was sitting on the front steps and watched a later Shepherd named Heidi maneuver my little sister in just such a way, her elbow riding on Heidi's back and her prattling away as the dog patiently walked her nearer to the house. In that moment it was as if I could feel the fur of a ghost-dog nudging my own side away from the road.

Rampant and lupine, these dogs loved to play tackle football,

tripping you up by snagging your cuff in their teeth. They caught baseballs and yellow jackets on the fly. They had a talent for fetching giant rocks, loving to wrestle the gallon-sized boulders, while drop-jawed I watched their struggles. With river turtles they could be delicate and scrupulous. With garter snakes they were uninterested. With skunks they were each curious at least once. With porcupines they were ferocious more than once and then I would watch my father snip the quills to relieve the pressure so to slip the barbs from noses and flews, the insides of mouths and pink gums, as these strong dogs submitted to his ministrations. With both skunks and porcupines, I remember my father scolding me for cruising the woods and getting the dog in

Labrador Retriever

Weimaraner

trouble. Such was their respected status in our house.

I could be brutal, but they endured. With equanimity they tolerated pulled tails and tugged ears and small hands inside their mouths. They were pillows and blankets or bodyguards with bared teeth and raised hackles, their spines curved and latent and a sound unearthly emanating from deep in their throats. In the '50s, there were transients who passed through when the weather was good. I remember no fear of child-snatchers, but some of the men would take up residence for a night in the hayloft, and my suspecting grandfather would call up to our house for my mother to bring the dog and chase them out. It was not that he was inhospitable, but he feared they might smoke, or drink, or do something stupid up there like die.

To think I was raised by these dogs is not so strange. I would have good reason to think this true. A boy's imagination naturally cleaves to stories of wolf-boys, and rightfully so. In all myth and

15

literature I have come to trust an iota of reality, however fragile. In all encounters with the fictional and the fantastic I assume a degree of historical imperative, and besides, being a fiction writer means that I rarely need make concessions to objective reality.

I remember too the cries when the Shepherds were old, or wrought with dysplasia, or used up from watching over us and no longer could stand. To this day I know where each is buried, their graves marked by lichened stone in sweeps of green fern. In another realm, one more civilized, these Shepherds would be the stationed ambassadors from the animal world. These dedicated beings are the sweet thought that light my remembering mind.

Bullmastiffs

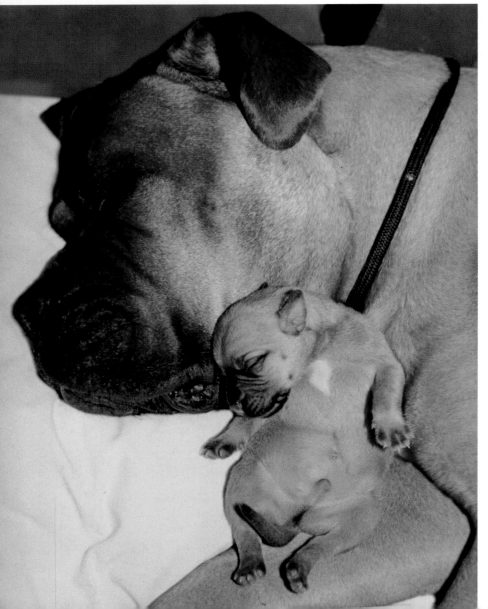

That weekend in November 1963, for all the tragedy and sadness, I confess I was overwhelmingly disappointed to the extent of childishness that there was nothing else on television but the unfolding sorrow of national grief. I was without much experience in life and still irresponsible. I had yet to become passionate. I had yet to reach the midlife peak of caring where the weight of living is measured in tons and your knees ache from it. I had yet to reach the age where a wandering thought of the past can make you shudder, and I wanted my weekend of cartoons.

My father was a Kennedy man. He became impatient with me and insisted that I watch and so under duress, I did. I watched the people pray on their feet and sing hymns

16

Boxers

skyward. I listened as men with hushed voices asked questions
they could not answer and still cannot, and so many years later
we experience a feeling of universal grief because with this death
did our dreams for ourselves seem so distant. I think back now:
1961 Ernest Hemingway, 1962 William Faulkner, 1963 John
F. Kennedy. A pretty bad run of luck for a country sorely in need
of no puny men, and the decade was just beginning. But I wonder, did the enormity of this dismaying act irreversibly define
reality or did it simply remind us of it?

If there was a photo of that week in 1963, it would be of me
sitting in my skivvies and in the chair beside me a German Shepherd Dog named Bullet and the both of us dutifully watching a
woman and her children bury the man who was to them husband
and father and to us an assassinated president. What the photo
would not show would be my whispering confessions into Bullet's
pointed ear, how I did not want to watch this black and white
pageant of grief and anguish. How I did not want to be missing
cartoons where creatures were shot, exploded, run down, throt-

tled, and clobbered and then stood up to be shot, exploded, run down, throttled, and clobbered all over again. That I could not watch this speedy reversible violence made me a whiny, churlish boy that weekend. Since then I have found dogs to be the best creatures for truth-telling and have yet to meet one that could not keep a secret.

Old English Sheepdogs

Now I have two English Setters, a 400-year-old breed, and one especially companionable. Before guns, men hunted with nets, and the setters were made to be handy dogs, holding the birds in their paws if they flushed. English Setters are still handy, touching at your face, or resting a paw on your arm and pressing for attention, or framing your head with their front paws while licking your face. They are cheeky and impertinent in their right to be personal. They expect to lie on the furniture and sleep on the bed. They like to perch on a chest or ride on shoulders, but when they are in the field they become demonic in their quest for birds, unbridled and nearly untamed, bordering control with pheasant lust, quail desire, and chukar joy. They embarrass themselves and it is to them and them alone I now confess my sins.

—*June 2002, "My Canine Confessor"*

Belgian Sheepdog

18

JANE SMILEY

My stepfather was a great man, and the greatest thing about him, as far as I was concerned, was that he wasn't afraid to bring home a puppy. He didn't ask permission of my mother, he didn't worry about the details. He just brought home the puppies and set them on the living-room floor, and he knew they would be taken care of, and they were. By the time my mother and I married into his family, I had had one dog, a cranky Cocker Spaniel named Christy who bonded only to my grandmother and didn't like children. She did not satisfy my longing for a dog (or a horse, my other great ambition). My new stepsister had almost done the trick. She'd been allowed to bring a puppy home from England, a miniature Poodle, silver, named Andre, but he was delicate and neurasthenic, and she was always calling him into her room as soon as I started petting him. In fact, I'm sure my mother and stepfather talked about this, because one day, when I was 11 years old, they brought

Dachshund

me into the family room during cocktail hour and there was a small, black Poodle puppy, and she was for me, and without even blinking I named her Phoebe. Phoebe was a real dog, a dog's dog. My stepsister liked Andre to have a nice show clip: topknot and bracelets and a full ruff. I remember looking at Andre's tiny refined toes and toenails with a measure of wonder. But Phoebe started with a puppy clip and stayed with a puppy clip, and that was really the best clip for her, because she spent all her days in the underbrush, killing small animals.

Dogs ran wild in those days, especially in the wealthier suburbs of St. Louis, where the houses were on three-acre lots and the roads, at least in our neighborhood, were mostly cul-de-sacs. Dog theory was much less sophisticated than it is now. They scratched to come in and they scratched to go out, and if you forgot to call them before you went to bed, you would awaken sometime in the night to the sound of them circling the house at a run and barking at the top of their lungs to be let in. They ate Hills Horsemeat from cans (which was much too rich for Andre, who should have been born in the era of designer dog food), and they were taught to sit, stay, and heel from a book of photos taken in 1940s New York. Phoebe was nonchalantly obedient. Her mind was elsewhere. What she really liked was for me to take her on long walks along the local creek. I would survey the autumn or the spring fields and trees and plan my future horse farm, and she would hunt. Did she eat what she killed? I can't remember, and possibly didn't notice. Once I saw her find a nest of baby rabbits under a tree and

Maltese

Opposite: Weimaraners

21

dispatch all three of the young, but then she turned away and continued on our walk, business as usual.

I liked the idea of sleeping with Phoebe, but once she grew out of puppyhood and became an outdoorsy, active dog, the reality was not quite what I had imagined, since St. Louis was tick central, and it was nearly impossible, even with regular tick baths, to keep up with them. I quietly decided to let her sleep with Andre in the dog room and have never really enjoyed having a dog in the bed from that day to this.

Both Phoebe and Andre, like all Poodles, excelled at jumping, and my favorite activity on the nights when my parents went out and the house was quiet was to set up obstacles made of mops and brooms and cans and boxes and jump the dogs over them—first getting them to sit-stay on the far side, then waving a Milk Bone and calling them over. Phoebe was more likely to slither through the jump, but this was Andre's métier, and he didn't mind either showing off or getting the reward that she didn't earn.

Belgian Tervuren

French Bulldog

I see dogs differently now—I have a blue Great Dane, a Golden Retriever, and a Jack Russell Terrier. They stay on their home territory and are well-behaved canines. Even the JRT has killed far fewer small animals than Phoebe did. We enjoy the dogs' personalities and idiosyncrasies in a way I didn't understand in those days, and they are more attuned to us. Phoebe was Phoebe was Phoebe, doing her thing, generally independent of the family. If we had all passed on, she would have been woolly and full of ticks, but self-sufficient, or that was the impression she gave. She chased cars, unheard of in a Smiley dog these days, and in the end, as they say, she caught one; the next puppy my stepfather brought home was a Vizsla.

I always say that a woman is lucky if in the course of her life she has one good man, two good horses, and four good dogs, and looking back, I know now that Phoebe was the first of my four.

—*June 2002, "The First Good Dog"*

Bearded Collie

PADGETT POWELL

A dog is the only friend you can have in life who will go with you wherever you want to go, whenever you want to go, without question and without putting on his pants. That is the quintessence of dog that secures our affection.

No questions, no pants, my dog, until he was killed at age 11 by a bobcat, was ready to go. He was capable of intimating that I was his first choice in traveling companion. No, that is inaccurate. You do not perceive in a dog the mechanism of choice, or preference, or judgement, or valuing one thing over another, and this is the second facet of the dog that wins us. He is coming with you because you are you. You? Let's go! With

Borzoi

Bulldog

Labrador Retriever

2 5

English Springer Spaniel

you, it's all good, he says, and you cannot help but love a thing that says that.

My dog would lead, get ahead by 50 feet, and select a fork in the trail and take it. If I paused at the fork, said, "Spode, this way," indicating the other fork, he would hustle back agreeably and take it. This was a complex, loveable moment: In it he said, Shucks! Alas, I presume! Goofy me! Shoulda known! You're right, boss! Better all around this way! And off he went down the path to the next fork, unabashedly presuming to pick a path there and repeat the little minuet of false humility if I again called him back. He'd do this all day, grinning.

My dog did not lie abed depressed. You don't get depression from a dog. A dog doesn't do down. This is the third magical facet in the bright furry diamond that a dog is. He's ready if you are, he's not wearing any clothes, and he's not depressed, and what on earth is better than that?

Basset Hound

Near the end, my dog did lie abed a bit longer when he heard a noise than he would have when young. He was 11, had no canines left, was partially paralyzed in the rear from weird coral-like ossifications on his lumbar vertebrae. So when the bobcat made its first unprovoked snarl just outside his house, he let it go. When the cat made a second horror-movie noise, it was too much. He got up, creaked out there, apparently engaged big cat with no teeth to engage it with, apparently got cut pretty badly, hiked about a third of a mile down some of our path forks to a place where fish die on our property after high water, bled copiously there on his good German-steel collar, was found there a week later with the help of buzzards, and had his bones recovered there six months later, which I bleached and

Dachshunds

Saluki

have boxed in a Rubbermaid Roughneck. It was not the worst day of his life. There was not a finer moment than confrontation, and there was not a finer thing to confront than an impossibly large cat—almost his size!—and if the cat prevailed, well, to him, that was another occasion for the grinning aw-shucks shrugging off of dubious judgement, so what. His collar is still in the woods, corroded by the salt in his blood to an inflexible rusty mass reminiscent of abandoned bicycle chain.

I recently was involved in the mercy killing of a bobcat struck by a car but not killed. When the game warden dispatched it with a neat, nearly invisible shot between the eyes, I took it to the taxidermist, paid $388.88, and now have it standing on two curious pieces of driftwood on my living room floor approximately over my dog's old house under our house. The cat looks like an agreeable fellow himself, and I wish we could walk the trails together, the three of us, and delight in meaningless corrections of the way to go.

—*September 2001, "Bright Furry Diamond"*

Bichon Frise

RICK BASS

Dogs live to be old, even ancient, in this green mountain valley of northwestern Montana. My old Black and Tan Coonhound from Mississippi, Homer, turned 16 this Easter and is now moving slowly but firmly into her seventeenth summer. I found her on the side of the road in 1985, with her sister (now deceased) and a third pup, roadstruck dead. I named her for Homer Wells, the orphan in John Irving's *The Cider House Rules.*

Homer herself has died several times, and yet each time somehow resurrects herself, though even I, her biggest fan, am forced to acknowledge that her miraculous powers of regeneration must surely be waning at this point in her life, her lives.

The first time she crossed over to the other side might not even have been a true death, but simply a sweet sleepiness. We were running down a trail at a state park in Mississippi, in the autumn. There was a low stone wall wandering through the woods, and running toward that wall at full speed, with young Homer beside me, I leapt over it, clearing it easily, and kept on going. Homer, however, for whatever reason, decided to try to run through the pile of autumn leaves that was stacked over and around the wall. There was some gap of dog logic that made her think, evidently, that because the wall in that one place was covered with raked-up leaves, and because leaves were soft, she could run right on through them.

When she hit the wall, she instantly bounced backward several feet, suddenly all loose-necked and rubbery-legged, and walked in one small circle—searching for me—before collapsing, out like a light. I ran to her, believing that she had passed on. It was several minutes before she came back to this side, and even then, was groggy for more than an hour.

The second time was more fully my fault. Trying to save money, I was worming her myself, rather than taking her to the vet. I was trying to feed her a big old horse-pill of cheap worm medicine, a blue gelcap the size of a locust, and understandably, she did not want to swallow it. Instead, she clacked it around in her jaws, gagging, then bit down, puncturing the gelcap and releasing into the room immediately the astringent odor of what smelled like turpentine. Her eyes began watering and she started to sneeze, and then went into convulsions as her blood filled with fiery vapors. She fell to the wooden floor, legs knocking and claws scrabbling, then shuddered—her eyes rolled all the way back—and then died, I am sure. I shouted for her to come back

Great Danes

31

English Cocker Spaniel

and gathered her up, rushed her out to the truck, and raced to the vet's office. And on the drive there, she resurrected.

She has been bitten by water moccasins so that her face has swelled to the size of a basketball and has been torn open by mountain lions and coyotes, only to come crawling back days later, entrails looping out. She has been in a fire tower that was struck by lightning and been bristle-filled with porcupine quills. She has fallen through the ice and has developed many a mysterious tumor, all of which have come to naught.

Last summer she encountered heatstroke—we had to bring her back by hosing her down and placing a fan in front of her. And this spring, after running hard up a hill through the tall dewy grass, tail wagging like a puppy—lunging, with her thick, old

Opposite: Labrador Retriever

32

heart, up that steep hill—she died at my feet, right as I turned to open the door for her.

One minute she was prancing in place, the way she does when she's ready and eager to come inside (breathing hard, it's true, but prancing) and the next moment she fell heavily to the ground, still and silent; and once again, her eyes rolled slowly back.

I called out her name again (useless; nearly blind and nearly deaf, she can hear only the highest-pitched whistle now) and stroked her head as I felt the life leaving her, and her muscles relaxing completely now, in death.

I kept petting her, sad and shocked that it had come this way; the end of two decades of her life, and mine. Always, you want one more day, to be kind, to be extra kind—and as I petted her, she woke up, then struggled to stand up, and then rose, wagging her tail, pleased as ever to be getting the attention.

Some mornings when I go out to her room she is sleeping so

Affenpinscher

34

Labrador Retriever

soundly, and in so loose and strange a sprawl that I think she has died in her sleep. And on those mornings, I get the impression that she has slept deeper, has dived deeper into the land of dreams, than she used to. That surely, now more than ever, the two worlds are blurring, and that she travels further and farther into a place where I can't go. That she is exploring that territory in the same manner which she has explored all of the woods and ridges around here for so many years. Checking it out.

I am reminded of the Mary Oliver poem "The Swan," with its lines

> . . . *Said Mrs. Blake of the poet:*
> *I miss my husband's company—*

Schipperke

> *he is so often*
> *in paradise . . .*

and

> *Oh, what will I do, what will I say, when those*
> *white wings*
> *Touch the shore?*

Where we buried her sister, Ann, there is a young aspen tree growing, which we planted five years ago when she died. There will one day be a second aspen there, slightly younger than the first, and as such, smaller. Sometimes I imagine that in her dives and her deaths, and in those sleeps of such profound depth, Homer, who has heard nothing but high whistles for so long now, somehow hears the green summertime rattling of those aspen leaves above, and then their drier, autumnal clattering, and that she imagines or knows that she is lying down warm in a patch of bare earth, within sight of the house she has not seen in a long time, but which she still knows intimately with the pads of her feet, and the rhythms of her memory.

But I don't know that. For all I know, when she goes over to the other side, each time, it is no different from this side—and though there might be no real reason to come back, still she does, every time, and greets me anew, each time, upon her return.

—*September 2001, "Homer the Earth Diver"*

DOUG MARLETTE

My wife and I have two Maltese. We named them Louie and Sophie, although sometimes I think we should have named them Testosterone and Estrogen.

Louie is all boy, playful and feisty, with a frizzy mop of unman-

Dalmatians, 1938

ageable hair and an adorable habit of cocking his head to one side to listen when he is spoken to. Sophie, in sharp contrast, enjoys being a girl. Demure and prissy, she is a true diva with beautiful, long, straight white bangs the color of corn silk.

Though they're both the size of Q-Tips, Louie swaggers with macho territoriality when we take them out for walks, barking at and straining on his leash toward dogs six times his size. Oblivious to the way the world sees him, he preens and struts, while Sophie, his girly-girl companion, is shy and self-conscious. Wary and skittish, she's more like a cat, really, than a dog—aloof, mysterious, and withholding, parsimonious with her affections and

Bloodhound

enthusiasms. Unlike Louie, who careens headlong wherever he goes, she moves daintily, with the carriage of a prima ballerina crossing a stage.

But different as they are, they are crazy about each other, frolicking together constantly, nipping and growling playfully. Sometimes, when swept up in his own manly man-ness, it slips Louie's mind that they have been spayed and neutered, and he tackles Sophie from behind. Sophie simply ignores this pointless display with looks of patience and forbearance.

When not wrestling or pitching woo, their days are spent draped over each other on our bed or on a pillow in their basket, or nestled like stoles over our shoulders while we read a book, or like comforters in our laps while we watch a video at night. At mealtime, they hustle to the kitchen and rear up on their hind legs like little circus performers dancing enthusiastically for doggy treats. Otherwise, entire days can be passed lying like throw pillows on the back of our living-room sofa, only occasionally rousing themselves to yap at the FedEx truck or any stranger passing on our quiet street. For basic couch spuds, they are excellent watchdogs, letting us know before a knock is heard or a doorbell chimes if someone has breached our doorway or airspace, although I wonder what good either would be if someone actually broke in, other than to cause the intruder to laugh himself to death.

Louie is especially devoted to our 14-year-old son, Jackson. If I try to hug my son or tousle his hair or interrupt his TV viewing with any gesture of spontaneous affection, fiercely vigilant Louie pounces on me, growling and barking ferociously.

Sophie, on the other hand, remains an exercise in frustration for Jackson, an object lesson in the feminine mystique and the irresistible allure of the unattainable. Naturally, he is smitten with her and, of course, she has him wrapped around her little paw. Intrigued by Sophie's maddening aloofness and charmed by her infinite indifference to him, he courts her, bribing her with doggy treats, laying her down on her back and rubbing her tummy just the way she likes it and, when all else fails, getting in her face and playfully blowing her bangs away from her eyes until she growls at him and occasionally even snaps at him. My wife and I have warned him not to be surprised if someday she takes off his nose.

Over time I have noticed that Louie has benefited from his time with the opposite sex, been civilized by the experience, grown smarter, wiser, deeper.

Likewise, Sophie has been drawn out of her shell, grown more affectionate, less defensive. Now Sophie even warms to Jackson and seeks him out for neck massages and tummy rubs. I know that his experience with über-female Sophie and the frustrations of unrequited love will serve him well as he moves into adolescence and the grownup battle of the sexes. I just hope he can keep his nose intact.

—*September 2001, "Testosterone and Estrogen"*

Here is a collie yarn that had been proven true. Many of you read of it in the newspapers. It will bear retelling:

A Montana restaurant man took his family and his eight-month collie pup, Bud, last summer for a motor trip to Indiana. While they were crossing Iowa, the collie wandered around during the family's lunch hour. He was caught by someone who was a better judge of dogs than of honesty. His owners would not find him. After a long search, they drove on to Indiana, and thence home.

The pup got loose and came rushing back to where he had left the car. It was gone. He followed it to Indiana, getting there just after his owner had set forth for Silverton, Montana. The pup started homeward in the wake of the car. How did he guess the route the car had taken to Indiana from Iowa, and thence to Montana? Nobody knows. But the testimony of garage-men and police along the line of travel proves he was seen in a score of places soon after the car had left those places.

At last, weary and footsore and thin and with his nails worn to the very quick, he limped into his master's restaurant near Silverton, Montana, and was wildly delighted to get home again. The young collie had traveled about 3,000 miles in all and had traversed seven wide states. How did he do it?

—July 1924, "And Speaking of the Collie"

Basset Hound

LBJ's Beagle, Him, and white Collie, Blanco, in the White House, 1965

DOGS
IN OUR
TIMES

Generations of our history are punctuated by good dogs at our sides.

Bull Terriers, circa 1939

The Hollywood dog roster is a famous one, and the stars' kennels bear many interesting titles that have never seen credit on the silver screen.

Undoubtedly, Harold Lloyd was among the first of the film celebrities to take up the banner of dogdom in earnest when he established his Great Dane kennels in West Los Angeles some years ago. There is an old saying that one should trust not in "a man who dislikes or who is disliked by dogs," and surely if this be true, Harold Lloyd is a prince among men, for every dog he has owned from the age of three until the present day has been completely devoted to the popular comedian, according to Mr. McGuire, his kennel master of some years standing.

When Lloyd was a small chap on a Colorado ranch, his uncle presented him with a dog named Bill, part mastiff and part Great Dane. This dog was his constant companion and protector, and when some years later Bill was poisoned, it was a great and never-to-be-forgotten blow to the little boy in Colorado.

Since that day, and until Lloyd was a grown man, famous in the film world, he was determined that sometime he would have many fine dogs—big dogs—like his old pal, Bill. Nor did he forget this promise to himself when fortune turned in his direction. With his first paycheck of any consequence, he purchased the best Great Dane he could find in the country, and before many more years had elapsed, his kennels had grown to 80 fine dogs—all Great Danes. Lloyd has gone through all the joy and sorrow of raising, breeding, and burying these pets. Scarcely a day goes by when he is in Hollywood and not in the throes of making a film that he doesn't find one excuse or another for spending at least a few moments at the kennels.

Of course, the best known Boston terrier in Hollywood is Patsy, the pet of the famous newspaper and radio film columnist Louella O. Parsons. Patsy is an aristocrat from the tip of her ears to the end of her stubby tail, and is extremely brilliant, according

Canine celebrities on the MGM lot, circa 1930

to her dog's mistress. Every morning Patsy sits at her feet in utter devotion while Miss Parsons grinds out her daily column and begs with all her might to accompany her in the car when she makes the rounds of the film studios.

—*February 1935,*
"Dogs That Love Hollywood Stars"

LEON F. WHITNEY

Today, so many thousands of dog lovers are wondering what they are going to do if this meat shortage continues.

Chihuahua

The shortage was partially one engineered by the Department of Agriculture of our government, and partially by nature. Droughts and dust storms would have been bad enough, and the reduction in the cattle population would also have been bad enough if either had come alone. The combination accounts for why we must pay 60 cents a pound for a juicy piece of steak for ourselves, or 15 cents a pound for beef for our dogs . . .

In my estimation, after many tests and study of all the available comparative tests, fish is fully as good a food for dogs as is meat. Of course, dogs do not readily take to it, but once they learn to, they love it. Fish can often be obtained in fresh form for very low prices. As I write this I can buy fresh mackerel for 4 cents a pound, and throughout the season, other varieties can be had for sometimes lower prices. In many nations, dogs are fed large amounts of fish, and they do very well on them.

—*November 1935, "Beating the Meat Shortage"*

USMC Devil Dogs in training, Camp Lejeune, North Carolina, 1943

COL. W.F.S. CASSON, D.S.O.

I could never find a satisfactory explanation for this sudden and amazing fidelity, except that perhaps either my scent or the tone of my voice may have resembled that of her former owner who may have been killed, or lost as she lost me only four months later.

For during that time she was practically never out of my sight: in the trenches, by day or night, through the hottest fighting, no matter where it was, she was always with me.

I well remembered how grateful I was for her warmth when snatching an odd hour's sleep during the Battle of Loos. Though the dugout was often rocking from the explosions of the shells close by, she slept unconcernedly.

She was well known in several divisions of the First Army, and also to some of the Germans, with, on one occasion, rather unfortunate results. She was a good ratter, and often killed one or two during my tour of the trenches. During these hunts, she would sometimes get on top of the parapet and over the other side, if I was not watching her, and it was not long before the Bosche tumbled to the fact that there were some brass hats going around when she was about.

—August 1936, "Some Dogs of Character"

FRANCIS V. CRANE

Don't let war hysteria get you down! Don't make the mistake that many did in England in the first year of the war when, from fear and anticipation of trouble to come, many put their pets to sleep needlessly, only to regret it shortly after. If a meat shortage does come, dogs can be kept well and healthy on a meatless diet. And surely there is no reason why we should expect a decrease in the supplies of biscuit, meal foods, vegetables, and slaughter-house by-products that can be used most successfully. So keep

FDR and Fala, Scottish Terrier, picnicking near Pine Plains, New York, 1940

your heads and don't become hysterical or act quickly, if any thoughts of destroying your pets come to mind.

—*January 1943*

ROBERT HANKS

One quiet Friday evening in the fall of 1951, Mrs. Lorrain D'Essen, owner of Dickie, received a frantic phone call from J. Cates, assistant director to comedian Jackie Gleason.

Opposite: The Collies of J. Pierpont Morgan with kennel master, circa 1904

50

"We understand you have a large dog that has been on TV," the voice said breathlessly.

"We," said Mrs. D'Essen, "have a Great Dane." Was he trained? . . . Yes, Dickie was trained.

Could she have him there within an hour? She did . . .

Dickie was not merely to be used as atmosphere—he had an actual part!

"You know, she said later they had no idea of how much they were asking or expecting of a dog." Besides making four entrances and four exits, Dickie had to greet a total stranger as a long-lost friend, sniff at a bowl of meat without eating it, look apologetically at a torn shirt, and at the end of the skit pull Gleason offstage on cue.

Dickie's sudden love and display of affection toward a man he had never seen before was accomplished by judiciously smearing the actor with liverwurst. Art Carney was the actor and a wonderful sport about it. The other bits had to be done by hand signals, given by Lorrain, out of audience and camera range from backstage. Lorrain's faith in Dickie was not misplaced, he came through like a true ham.

At the break of the show Jackie Gleason came over and glowed with enthusiasm at the wonderful performance of the dog and the remarkable handling from backstage. This show encouraged Lorrain to further the use of animals through her; this became a reality when they called on Lorrain for the services of a variety of dogs and many repeats with Dickie. So was born something new under the TV sun.

—*February 1953, "Something New Under the TV Sun"*

The introduction of detector dogs on a broad scale, as a major tool in the stepped-up drive on narcotic smuggling along the borders and at the country's major gateways, was announced by U.S.

Commissioner of Customs Myles J. Ambrose.

The program is part of the crackdown mounted on June 1, by the Bureau of Customs, an arm of the Treasury Department, on drug smuggling. The drive is directed principally against hard drugs such as heroin and cocaine, but is also aimed at interdicting the large-scale smuggling of marijuana and hashish, the use of which has reached epidemic proportions.

Detector dogs have been tested by the Customs Service for several years. They have proved their effectiveness in the location of marijuana and hashish (its concentrated derivative), particularly in mail parcels and cargo sent to the United States from abroad, and in vehicles at border stations . . .

Training for each dog and handler takes approximately two months. Initially, Customs officers instruct the handler in Customs laws, procedures, and search techniques. Then a training program matching each dog handler with two dogs is set up. During this phase, the dogs learn to find and point out concealed marijuana and the handler learns to respond to each dog's method of alerting him.

Before graduation, the dogs must successfully complete intensive tests, including finding marijuana concealed among parcels of foodstuffs and disguised by odor-masking chemicals. In one of

President and Mrs. Hoover and their German Shepherd Dog, 1932

the tests, marijuana is buried in a fruit jar under a gravel road. The dog must walk along the road, locate the jar, and dig it up.

—*December 1970, "Detector Dog Program"*

Buddy, Bill Clinton's recently acquired chocolate Labrador Retriever (the most popular breed of 1997), has probably settled into everyday life at the White House by now. Socks, the Clintons' beloved cat, may still have some reservations, however, about her new housemate.

—*April 1998, "The President and His Buddy"*

GEORGE BERGER

The final editing, art, and production work for this issue were done the week of September 11, the most difficult, frightening, and longest week in many of our lives. The distractions and turmoil were almost too hideous to bear. Those of us who work and live in the New York area suffered a particular agony. Hardly any of us would not lose a friend or relative, nor escape the torment of the less personal but nonetheless devastating implications of the entire series of terrors.

Our common reaction to that Tuesday's news was to flee, to shut down our senses, to get away from the grotesque words and images that were exploding before our very eyes.

But it didn't take long to realize that, no, we weren't going to run away from it at all. We would absorb it, try our best to understand, and then, in keeping with our national character, move forward. We would get the job done, however grand, however menial.

In the end, does publishing a magazine, or the sport of dogs, have the importance of the ghastly loss of lives we've witnessed

A persistent Terrier in a popular TV commercial of the 1970s

Basset Hounds

or the wicked threat to our American way of life? Certainly not. What is important, though, is that we stay the course, not be cowed by diseased, criminal minds, not alter our personal or professional missions, whatever they may be.

—*October 2001, "Publisher's Note"*

BUD BOCCONE

"I have a 38-officer command," says Lt. Dan Donadio of the New York City Police Department K-9 Unit as he leads the way to the kennel, "but I like the dogs better. They don't argue." During his 19 years on the force, the lieutenant, of Staten Island by way of Bensonhurst, Brooklyn, has perfected the world-weary authority and needling humor typical of his profession.

His domain is a remote patch of asphalt on the Brooklyn

waterfront. The facilities are Spartan: a cluster of stationary double-wide trailers that serve as offices, a chain-link kennel, a makeshift agility course, and a soda machine. Nothing fancy, nothing cute. No one does Spartan like the NYPD. But seven days a week, day and night, this forlorn-looking outpost deploys highly skilled dog-and-handler teams to the city's five boroughs in response to calls for virtually every kind of K-9 police work: search and rescue, tracking-trailing, subway patrol, field and building searches, criminal apprehension.

"These are some of the best-trained, best-maintained police dogs in the world," says Donadio proudly as he inspects his charges. "Each dog is certified monthly by New York State to ensure they're at their absolute peak physically and temperamentally." They sure look it: A row of bright-eyed, beautifully condi-

Bull Terrier star Wildfire in 1917 MGM silent feature The Bar Sinister

Labrador Retriever

tioned German Shepherd Dogs are in their runs. There's Billy, Loki, Ricky and . . . a litter of kittens?

"Yeah, the cat who hangs around here had them. We're trying to find them good homes," explains the lieutenant. "Since this unit was formed in 1980 we've never destroyed a healthy animal, and we're not starting now. My wife and I already have three at home, and I'm allergic. So, if you know anyone who'd like a kitten . . ."

—*October 2000, "NYPD True"*

Since the death of Jacqueline Kennedy Onassis on May 19, Americans have been taking a mental inventory of their memories of this timeless first lady. One of them is former secretary of the AKC, A. Hamilton Rowan, who remembers the day in 1969 when Onassis visited 51 Madison with her son John Jr. to receive the official registration certificate for his English Cocker Spaniel, Shannon Kennedy.

When Onassis and her son visited the AKC to retrieve the

Golden Retriever

German Shepherd Dog

Yorkshire Terrier Smoky, named Best Mascot of the Pacific Theater by Yanks Down Under magazine, on the front in New Guinea in World War II

Cocker's papers, Rowan presented the offical registration papers along with a three-generation pedigree and a copy of *The Complete Dog Book* to the young boy, and proceeded to take mother and son on a two-hour tour of the company, occasionally stopping by the desks of flabbergasted employees for brief introductions.

When Rowan rode the elevator with Onassis and John Jr. back to the lobby, a crowd of some 200 people were waiting there to catch a glimpse of the elusive first lady.

—*July 1994, "Jacqueline Onassis Remembered"*

Early in the morning, on my way to the office, I often encounter a parade of purebred dogs within my five-block radius of the AKC. So, during a recent weekend, with no shows to take me away from Manhattan, I took some photographs of these early birds and added a few more on a Sunday visit to Central Park. Although most of them are neither the greatest representatives of their respective breeds, nor in what would be considered perfect show condition, they command my respect and attention. City dogs, somehow, have a dignity and bearing no matter how humble their origins that set them apart from their country cousins. They are generally a no-nonsense group, going about the business of escorting their masters on the end of the lead, patiently waiting tied to a parking meter outside the store marked NO PETS, PLEASE, and keeping a sharp eye on the flow of traffic. My particular street dogs have lovely dispositions and almost all, according to their owners, are AKC registered.

—*September 1981, "On the Sidewalks of New York"*

"I guess that applying for the registration is up to Charlie Brown, isn't it?" Charles M. Schulz asked when visited by the GAZETTE. "He knows who his mother and father are, although the Daisy Hill Puppy Farm doesn't exist anymore. It's now a five-story parking lot."

—*December 1979, Editor's Note*

What's so new about the Beatles' haircuts, anyway? Irish Waters have been wearing their hair that way for over 100 years!

—*November 1964, Irish Water Spaniels breed column*

MRS. CHARLES FORREST DOWE

One of the most sincere dog lovers I know is Gov. Thomas
E. Dewey of New York. This summer we had the great pleasure
of spending a weekend with him at his lovely farm high in the
rolling hills of Pawling, N.Y. Should Gov. Dewey attain the highest public office that can be offered to any citizen, I well know
that the halls of the White House will echo with the sounds of
happy dogs. Gov. Dewey is never too busy to lose contact with
the animals on his large farm and he is "a natural" with dogs. He
never passes a dog without a word of greeting, which is returned
by a wagging tail.

—October 1948

CLAYTON G. GOING

Bulldogs, circa 1900

Dear Editor: War is a grim business in which sentiment plays little
part. But one of the most touching things in this global
conflict is the complete mutual devotion, confidence, and
understanding that exist between America's war dogs and
their handlers.

Such was the relationship of Marine PFC Robert E.
Lansley of Syracuse, and Andy, an affectionate, alert
Doberman Pinscher, formerly owned by Theodore A.
Wiedemann of Norristown, Pa. Lansley and Andy went
through months of bitter fighting on Bougainville where
the Devildog's keen nose repeatedly saved Marines from
certain and sudden death by discovering camouflaged Jap
machine-gun nests. He was cited for his heroism.

Then, one tragic night, Lansley wrote to his mother this
letter—a Marine's simple, yet beautiful tribute to his dog:

*Dear Mom: My heart is wide open. My Andy is gone.
The darn mutt got out and as he couldn't hear because*

64

of deafness brought on by the shelling he was run over by a truck.

I got the worst order the Marine Corps ever imposed on me. I had to destroy my Andy.

To think, Mom dear, he saved my life and I had to take his. No matter how many dogs they give me, I'll never have the faith in them that I had in Andy. It seems that he was my other self.

Smooth Fox Terrier and Doberman Pinscher installation into Veteran K9 Corps, 1945

Bob and his Andy are now together again. The Marine was later killed in action fighting on the island highway to Tokyo.

—*July 1945, "The Postman's Whistle"*

WALLACE REYBURN

With the Canadians in Italy—Announcement has just been made of an ingenious method we have evolved for combating the dogs the Germans are using on the Canadian front to hamper the patrols. We have pressed into service female dogs who happen to be in an amorous mood. They don't do anything in particular.

65

Champion Wire Fox Terrier arriving from England, 1947

They are just around the place. The German dogs are deserting the enemy lines for ours in droves.

—*October 1944, "Coast to Coast Clips"*

PEORIA STAR

A patriotic canine is Bing, who brings home tin cans the way other dogs bring bones. Whether or not he read the newspapers or just happened to hear about the big tin can salvage effort in Peoria is unrevealed, but he carries his quota home from the neighborhood daily, to be added to the cans collected here for war production. Appropriately enough, he is a soldier's dog, belonging to Pvt. William Bietz of 514 State Street, who is away at Jefferson Barracks, Mo. The fact that he can find the cans to bring home is evidence that not all Peoria housewives are contributing theirs to the salvage drive.

—February 1943, "Coast to Coast Clips"

FREEMAN LLOYD

The earliest of the Clumber spaniels were first owned by Prince Albert, husband of Queen Victoria. These were the great-great-grandparents of the present heir presumptive to the throne, Princess Elizabeth, undoubtedly one of the most beloved of all the younger English ladies who go in for dogs.

The princess positively dotes on her Pembroke corgis, and there is every reason to believe it is her "fancy" for the breed that has made, and will continue to make, the Welsh farm dogs splendidly and increasingly popular on both side of the Atlantic.

It was not so long ago, when seeing off a friend voyaging on the Queen Mary, that I was told that Princess Elizabeth was not only well-acquainted with the names of some of the winning corgis in America, but the names of their owners as well. In which way might such information reach Buckingham Palace, London, it was asked.

"Oh," replied Mrs. Lewis Rossler, "my friend, Mrs. Phil Gray, owner of the famous Rozavel Kennels, after she had been over

New York Mayor Ed Koch with Sarah Jessica Parker and terrier mix Sandy, stars of the Broadway musical Annie, 1979

German Shepherd Dog,
World War II

here judging corgis was asked to call and pass an opinion on some of the princess's dogs of that breed, and about American dogs."

"May I ask how is it you know so much about American dogs?" the visitor enquired.

"I've copies of the AMERICAN KENNEL GAZETTE. I'll fetch and show them to you. They're up in my room."

Forthwith, Princess Elizabeth scampered off and returned with the magazines with their displays of corgi pictures and descriptive letterpress. But, perhaps, the best point of this intimate story concerning present-day English royalty and its dogs was kept by the fair narrator for the last moment, when the "All Ashore That's Going Ashore" was signaled by voice and hooter.

"And Mrs. Gray begged that I tell you, the GAZETTES were well-thumbed."

—*June 1939, "The Royal Dogs of Britain"*

Opposite: Beagles

In his recent lecture in Exeter, Eng., on Capt. Scott's expedition, Mr. C. H. Meares mentioned that in his forthcoming expedition Sir Ernest Shackleton would take a number of dogs which had been used for hauling in Canada. The animals, numbering ninety-nine, arrived in London, and will leave again on the *Endurance*. They are all half-breeds, their ancestry being represented by wolves, and have been used for sleighing and hauling fish. Fish has been their chief food, but in view of the special work for which they are destined they have been trained to feed on biscuits—quite a new form of sustenance to them until they left Montreal for London, but so acceptable that they consumed 18 cwt. of Spratt's Meat Fibrine Dog Cakes by the time they arrived, and are now confirmed biscuit eaters. That they should have taken so readily to their new food is fortunate, for more depends on this than may be imagined. Captain Scott admitted that his failure to reach the Pole on his 1901 expedition was due to the fact that he substituted stockfish for biscuits as food for the dogs which accompanied him on his final dash. Sir Ernest Shackleton will rely on Spratt's Dog Cakes for his teams' food, and a sufficient supply is being taken on board the *Endurance* to last throughout the expedition.

—*June 1916, "Dogs for South Pole"*

*Dalmatian coach dog,
circa 1935*

San Antonio *Gazette*: By the peculiar howling of a Scotch collie dog, owned by W. Jay DeLamater, of 432 Magnolia Avenue, at 4:36 o'clock this morning, a fire alarm was given that awoke people for a distance of four blocks from the scene of the blaze and prevented what might have been a complete destruction of the entire block and the loss of life.

—October 1909, "Good for the Collie"

W. RULOFF KIP

One morning came to me Summer Mountain, my courier, while we were waiting in Tokyo for the Yokohama steamer, and suggested that we take home a pair of "Chin" dogs, or Japanese dogs, but as I had not seen any of them in Japan the thought of bringing home a pair had not occurred to me, or any of us, in fact.

"They are very nice little dogs," said Summer Mountain. "All Japanese ladies have 'Chin' dogs."

"But we are not Japanese ladies, or any other kind of ladies," I protested. "We are three men."

U.S. Coast Guard dogs, 1943

"You can give them to some ladies at home," continued the crafty Oriental. "Now that photograph you have always on your bureau, that is surely not your estimable mother—"

"Get them," I said. "Say not more." After he was gone I regretted my decision. "Three men and two ladies' dogs," I sighed.

Summer Mountain appeared next day in his rickshaw with a bird cage on his lap, and when the pie was opened two little black-and-white puff balls rolled out and began to sing.

"That little one, female, very good 'Chin,'" explained Akiyama (which is Japanese for Summer Mountain); "Fuji, the dog, too big," he continued, "but they make a very good pair."

And the next day the passengers of the *Empress of India* were edified by the sight of three strong men, accompanied by their servant, bearing a cage containing two ladies' lap dogs. They were, nevertheless, the pets of the ship, and divided honors with a pair of large Chinese "Chows" belonging to a lady.

—*October 1902, "How Rhinebeck Fuji*
and Rhinebeck Chindi Came from Japan"

Fanciers' Gazette: In imitation of other Continental armies, that of Austro-Hungary is being provided with trained dogs. The report came from Bosnia that the other day one of these soldier-dogs carried a message over a distance of eight miles in an hour and five minutes. The sheep dog, the poodle, and the pointer are the breeds found most suitable for military training. The duties of the war dogs are to carry dispatches and ammunition, and to guard depots. They also perform outpost duty. Among the new agents of modern warfare the dog is likely to prove neither the least useful not the least formidable.

The Austrians are imitating the Russians and Germans. But these are not the originators of the practice; they have simply revived it, for the dog of war is a most ancient institution. In the ranks of Colophon and of the Gastebeles dogs went to war with men. There was not a Greek fortress unguarded by dogs, and in the Poecile of Athens, alongside of the warrior men of Marathon, were pictures of warrior dogs that fought by their side in battle. Cyrus employed dogs of war, so did the Hyrcanians, the Magnesians, and the Paonians. The King of Garamantes employed an army of dogs to reconquer his throne, and the most important outpost of Corinth consisted of fifty terrible dogs of war. All the world knows how they saved the city on that dread night when the garrison was drunk—how the enemy landed, how the beasts attacked them and fought like lions, how nine-and-forty of the guards fell dead on the field of battle, how the dog Soter, perceiving that he alone was left alive, turned tail, fled, woke the soldiers, and thus saved Corinth. The dogs of Corinth probably wore mail like those figured on the bronze found at Herculaneum, and now in the museum of Naples.

—*November 1889,*
"Dogs in War Time"

This Week: We now know from an impeccable source, what the president wants to do when he leaves the White House: raise and breed Scotties. And he intends to breed

Saint Bernard, Beggar, and three-year-old master rescued from drowning, 1962

National
Dog Hero
of
Heroes
FIRST PLACE
BEGGAR
1962

them chiefly for personality. Like Fala. The only detail our friend didn't get was when F.D.R. plans to begin.

—July 1944, "Coast to Coast Clips"

OTUS RENARD

Dalmatian

Daisy, the most publicized dog in the world, is probably the only canine female impersonator. For years, his clever antics in the "Blondie" series have been enjoyed by movie fans who believed him to be a her. During the filming of *The Women*, MGM studios ballyhooed the "fact" that like the stage play of the same name, no one in the cast, including the animals was a male. Then, just as the picture was nearing completion, a bright lad discovered Daisy's true sex much to the consternation of the publicity department. This unfortunate and embarrassing disclosure was effectively hushed up at the time.

—May 1940, "Daisy Is Hollywood's Only Dog Female Impersonator"

Rat-tat-tat barked a chorus of machine guns. Although it was deep night, the sky overhead was a purplish canopy of bursting shells. Uncle Sam was beginning to throw the full force of his western energy against the overflowing German trenches. The doughboys were not without casualties, and Red Cross units worked long hours, carrying back the wounded as lumbering motor lorries, thundering over the pitted roadways, advanced fresh troops to the forward lines.

There could be no flinching under such conditions. "Carry on" was the only word to come from the pain-pinched lips of the stricken and torn, khaki-clad men. It was in such a Hell that Gamin—not a man in muddy uniform of cloth, but a light-colored sable shepherd, muddy enough—was giving his best in the service of mercy.

Gamin—having the speed of a devil and the heart of an angel—continually took supplies and messages across shot-riddled expanses where men would never dare to go. Time and again it was only the grit and loyalty of the canine soldier that saved his master from destruction. But these were not his greatest deeds.

It was in the great and successful drive of 1918, with wounded warriors pouring into the first-aid stations, that P.A.B. Widener and his orderly started to a Red Cross base with a motor ambulance filled with tortured men. As they were flying fast and silently along the danger-teeming road, an unannounced shell landed too closely, and, upturning the car, left Mr. Widener and the other occupants stranded and incapacitated.

Hours passed. It seemed as though the men would perish in the open. Then it was that Gamin played his ace. Following his unfailing sense of smell, the dog led a searching party straight to the master whom he loved.

For saving lives of those stranded men Gamin later was

rewarded. When the big strife ended, Mr. Widener brought the faithful animal home to live in royal splendor at Elkins Park. Later he was sent to Kentucky as a guard for the breeding stables of race horses owned by J. E. Widener, and there he is today.

—September 1924,
"Dogs That Dwell in Marble Halls"

JOHN BILLINGS JR.

If on a sunny spring morning you walk down Executive Avenue, between the White House and the Treasury Building, Washington, you will doubtless see President Coolidge's two dogs on the lawn inside the high picket fence of the chief executive's mansion. One is a white Scotch collie named Rob Roy. The other, an Airedale puppy, is Paul Pry, formerly known as Laddie Buck.

If you stand at the iron railing which encircles the White House grounds and whistle coaxingly, Rob Roy and Paul Pry will pause in their playful frisking to give you a questioning glance. They would not bark at your intrusion; they are too well-mannered for that. But they are a little suspicious of strangers. They lead sheltered lives under the shadow of the White House and are not in the habit of making friends too readily through the iron fence.

A president is known by his dogs. On entering the White House scores of breeders offer him the pick of their kennels. He makes his choice and thereon much depends. The country at large takes a natural interest in the president's dogs and judges him by the taste and discrimination he shows in his selection. Not least among the causes for the popularity of the late President Harding was his Airedale, Laddie Boy, and the deep attachment which bound them together. Everybody liked Laddie Boy, and this feeling redounded in favor of Laddie Boy's master.

—April 1924, "A President Is Known by His Dogs"

The New York Times: A small fortune is represented in the eight or ten little dogs that make their home at the St. Regis, and any bright afternoon it is no uncommon sight to see the little canine aristocrats out for an airing, each in charge of a maid, who, in apron and cap, exerts as much care and caution in watching over her charge as is ordinarily bestowed upon a baby.

Yesterday afternoon eight of these maids were parading up and down Fifty-fifth Street in front of the hotel, each leading a dog by a leash. All the dogs seem to be on good terms with one another and were interested in a large Angora cat huddled up discreetly in the arms of the maid who had it in charge.

One maid said the little woolly dog in her care, breed unknown to its keeper, was the property of Miss Francis Carolan, and that it is worth "its weight in gold."

—*January 1909, "Every Dog Has Its Maid"*

Labrador Retriever

RICHARD SCHICKEL

Movie dogs are like human movie stars in one important respect: They are ideal representations of their species. They are (or at least appear to be) just a little more handsome, a little smarter, and a lot braver than average. Beyond that, dog stars are spared the downside of human stardom, which is the awful knowledge that they are stars.

—*September 2001, "Lights, Camera, Dogs!"*

Afghan Hound

THE
SPORT
OF DOGS

They thrive on competition, for no reward other than to hear "Good Dog!"

Cardigan Welsh Corgi

It is the end of another long summer day. The lengthening shadows signal that the time has come to gather the flock from the fields for the evening. The sound of an occasional distant bleat from the farmyard encourages the woolly stragglers in as the shepherd walks through the lush pasture, directing his faithful canine companion to this last task of the evening.

A quiet rustling in a nearby grove of trees, nearly inaudible to the human shepherd's ear, instantly draws the attention of the Border Collie away from the ewes already gathered in the field. It is an inherited knowledge passed down by generations of working ancestors that tells the dog with no uncertainty that his work in this pasture is not done.

His body easily drops into a tense pose, not unlike that of a silent predator stalking its prey. All movement ceases in the field as his intense, mesmerizing gaze locks onto something seen only by his keen eye. One foot hovers gracefully above the grass, ready for the slightest call to action.

It is this moment that he lives for, that his entire existence is based upon. It comes so easily to him, this uncanny ability to unlock the hidden thoughts of the wooled creatures standing before him. A strong instinct guides him as he anticipates and controls their every move with calm, efficient precision. Although the sheep react with uncertainty at first, the two species quickly and quietly develop a mutual respect.

With the help of his master, the fleet-footed guardian of the flock collects the last of the lingering ewes. The desire that leads him is a desire like none other. It is impossible to watch a herd-

Papillon

Vizsla

ing dog in this element without being awed by the wonder and mystery of it all.

Truly, the greatest reward at the end of the day is a pat on the head by a gentle, weathered hand and a soft "Good job, boy. That'll do, lad. That'll do."

—*August 1999, "The Call to Action"*

BRAXTON B. SAWYER

The unprecedented growth of the dog show in the United States has crowded the ringsides with a new look. These eager and enthusiastic exhibitors and spectators are asking questions. "How did the idea of a dog show get started?" "Who staged the first show?" "Where was it held?" "Who judged it?" "Who got Best in Show?" These, and dozens other kindred questions are asked every week around dog shows all across the country . . .

—*May 1970, "Origin of the Dog Show"*

E. J. LEWIS

A dog show is an educational institution. Much may be read in books concerning dogs. Doubtless something may be learned from them. But a real canine education can be acquired only by experience with an observation of them in actual life, and nothing has yet been devised which can compare with a dog show for furnishing that observation and experience.

—*November 1946, "What Is a Dog Show?"*

ARTHUR FREDERICK JONES

Outside, a morning wind wrapped its cold, white garments around a city whose customary roar was so muted that its very identity seemed changed. Buses and taxicabs and a scattering few private motorcars poked their way cautiously through the smothering pelter of snow and sleet, their running lights so crusted as to seem no brighter than the glow of dying fireflies.

Inside, a vast throng sat around a brightly lighted arena, watching a spectacle that had been unfolded for countless other crowds in other days. These people had come to Madison Square Garden in New York to see the crowning of another outstanding

Chesapeake Bay Retriever

Bloodhounds

dog; of a dog that could take its place beside all the greats of Westminster history.

It hardly seemed that there was any connection between what was taking place indoors, under such festive, normal conditions, and the blizzard that was raging just outside the walls. And yet, to some, there was deep significance in that blanket of snow dripping so swiftly around the Garden and the ordinarily noisy City of New York.

Down under the floodlights of the Garden were six of the

finest specimens of purebred dog that ever have trod into a final ring at a dog show. They could not all win; nor could they all show that measure of perfection which the judge, Dr. Samuel Milbank, saw in the black Cocker Spaniel, Ch. My Own Brucie. To Brucie went the highest honor among 2,738 specimens sent to New York and Westminster from all corners of the North American continent.

—March 1940, "Westminster"

No one, we think, who can look back 20 years will deny that dog shows have been of the greatest service in establishing types

Pharaoh Hounds

of the different breeds and setting up standards of excellence for breeders. In former days, when 16 or 20 dogs came into the ring, it was an easy matter to pick out the prizewinners and to dismiss the rest. Now, of course, it is not an uncommon thing to find as many dogs before the judge, and not a bad one in the class. This improvement has come about through dog shows in various ways: First, judges questioned by anxious and disappointed exhibitors have generally been ready to explain what judging meant, and what was required. Many a kindly and useful answer have we had from judges, and many most useful hints have we picked up from them. Exhibitors and visitors, too, have been thrown together, and have learned that breeding and judging are not pure matters of luck and fancy, and that much matter of scientific interest may be learned in the amusement of breeding dogs.

—*January 1891, "What Dog Shows Have Done"*

Dalmatian

DAVID S. EDGAR JR.

Back in the spring of 1929, before the crash of October took all the money out of circulation, a very nice and totally unexpected win made a fanatic out of me . . .

So, in my frenzied enthusiasm, overcoming the poverty I shared with all the world, I kept breeding and exhibiting. I had had dogs long before that time, hunted with many of them, and exhibited a few. But my organized participation began only then.

Before that, my activities had lacked in logic. They began years earlier with a fox terrier which ran rabbits; a collie which merely tried to do so, but succeeded in becoming a fair coon dog under another teacher; and an abortive bear hunt with an Airedale. On that occasion, I nearly shot a dark-garbed linesman working at the base of one of the poles of a high tension system across a Catskill range. He looked, for all the world, like Bruno on his hindlegs.

Later came the win which infected me, and a little later, my first championship, which is as big a thrill as it is supposed to be.

However, the greatest experience of all is the first litter of purebreds.

It came before I began to show in earnest—even before the fatal win. Thisbe was in that litter.

Since 1929, I think I have played this dog game with the beginnings of intelligence. I certainly have played it with a great

Border Collie

Old English Sheepdog

deal of passion, and my partners complain that I've sometimes neglected my law practice in the process. I've hardly missed a show within 500 miles of New York.

What a pastime it is!

The years of my activity were the present "depression years," yet during these dark days, registrations, in breed after breed, have climbed steadily upward. Likewise, I have seen show after show with little or no falling off in entries, some with large increases, and very few shows suspended. I have received higher prices for puppies during these lean years than ever before, though that experience may have been merely unusual luck.

—*October 1933, "Take It From Me, It's a Great Game"*

Chesapeake Bay Retriever

GEORGE BERGER

You might spend hours, godawful long hours, in that marsh. Anybody who chirps about it all being a good time— well, you have to wonder about the quality of their existence. It can be boring to the point where, just for entertainment, you try to name the capitals of all 50 states. Or intone the starting lineup for the 1987 World Champion Minnesota Twins. Some entertainment.

But boredom, after all, is manageable. It's the cold and wind—treacherous co-conspirators-that can do you in. They come missiling across the open water, seeking flesh. Leave a quarter-inch of skin exposed and you are, in the words of state hunting and fishing guides, "at peril." Packing it in, heading for home, calling it a day—all become tempting concepts.

The Lab, of course, disagrees. He is in his element, shivering only with anticipation. The miraculous chemistry of his double coat allows him to stand statue-still against the ice-filled gusts. We've long known how much keener his senses of smell and hearing are than ours. And there may be something else, a

Opposite: West Highland Terrier

mystery sense foreign to human experience, that puts him on priority-alert.

He is focused minutes before you hear a thing or see even the tiniest flying speck. Then, heartbeats later, the birds break through the gray screen of sky. Honking. Screaming. Wings pounding. The dog's great head follows them intensely. No other part of him moves. He is well-trained, obedient, loving and loyal, but now neither command, nor whistle, nor thwack on the rump can distract him. This is the time when nothing else matters. And at this moment, in this single magnificent retriever, you understand what there is to know about purpose, and life.

Border Collie

—*August 1999, "When Nothing Else Matters"*

SARAH M. GREENHOW

The reason a big dog show like Westminster draws so many spectators is not because there are famous champions competing. No, the big magnet is usually furnished by the dog, big or little, that is pining away at home for his master or mistress. Said master or mistress may or may not—usually the latter—know a Truf-

Opposite: Collie

fle Hound from a Tahltan Bear Dog, but he or she has a continual and persistent interest in how good dogs look at their best. The reason? Simply so that he or she may go home, take his or her own pet, Rover, fondly by the ears and confide: "You look far better to me than all those champions."

—*March 1947, "Next to Godliness"*

Portuguese Water Dog

LOUISE SPRAGUE

Out of the same fat cornucopia of scientific goodies that has already spilled so many other delightful morsels as contributions to our way of life comes a tidbit that the world of dogs in particular and dog lovers in general should relish fully—the television dog show. The first presentation of this kind was of an experimental nature and took place on July 30, 1943, at WRGB, General Electric's station in Schenectady, N.Y., but this test worked out so well that another canine production was sent over the air waves shortly thereafter. In both cases, usual dog show procedure was followed with few variations—these for the most part to increase audience interest rather than because of technical limitations.

Not that the television dog show is without limitations, for it may be a long day before fanciers realize their dream of being able to sit at home of a weekend and, by thumbing the dial of their receiving set, bring in the views and the sounds of any important bench show in the nation. Such a pleasant state of affairs must remain, for a while, as a hope rather than a definite expectation . . .

—*December 1943,*
"Dog Shows for Shut-Ins"

JOHN KEMPS

Ever since the firm of Hitler, Hirohito, and Benito, Inc., tried to open an office at Pearl Harbor, many specialty and show-giving clubs have been split as wide open as Adolf's declaration that he and his business associates intended

German Wirehaired Pointer

to take "the world for their oyster" and put it in their own exclusive brand of stew. The clubs in question have split over debates as to whether or not it is patriotic to hold shows in competition with the "biggest show on earth," which, we all agree, should be and will be to show the international firm we

Alaskan Malamute

have mentioned the door and help them make a rapid and undignified exit.

—January 1943, "Match Shows Have a Mission"

C. W. GUSEWELLE

It was about 100,000 years ago, DNA analysis suggests, that the Asian wolf began its long, long journey toward participation in the Westminster Kennel Club Dog Show.

Then, somewhere in the Middle East, likely in the area now known as Iraq, his path and ours converged. The wolf-dog came into the cave where our Neolithic forbears were chipping flint points, and we fashioned a coexistence beneficial for us both. We worked together and hunted together, and over time—much time—the dog, a protean creature, took on the fabulous variety of shapes we know today.

Mankind, too, became domesticated, concerned with his cholesterol and the vesting of his pension. But something else had happened along the way. Our partnership of convenience is different now, and more—a kinship, you might almost say, rooted in bonds of devotion on both our parts.

The sorrow is that, although their history, like ours, is long, their lives are short. I've mourned other good dogs and other dear friends. But none any more keenly, I have to say, than I mourn my old bird dog Rufus as another autumn starts to turn.

I might claim that in his prime he was the finest quail dog ever.

Border Collie

But there isn't a hunter who wouldn't say that about the one great pup of his life, and each of them would be telling the absolute truth. Memory colors everything, and memory can't be entirely trusted. So it's important to try to speak of things surely known.

Rufus was a Brittany, from proven hunting stock. His sire was a Missouri dog named Winchester Repeater; his dam, Rosanna, was from the Kansas Flint Hills. His registry name was Rufus of Robins Hill. Almost from the day he joined us he was a recurring character in my column for the *Kansas City Star.*

I write at home, and my "office" is my wife's flower room on the side of the house. Rufus claimed the couch there. Besides being my partner in the field, he was my companion while I worked—more civil company, and better behaved, than you're apt to find most days in a newsroom.

All his milestones were celebrated in print: his puppy interest in a quail wing hidden at the edge of the lawn; his first point and first retrieve; one fabulous morning of 18 coveys of birds, four of them in a single half-mile hedgerow. Other days of few quail but much happiness—the grass frosty underfoot and autumn leaves

Greyhound

blown on a sharp, clean wind. Lunches he and I shared afield; the companionship of good dogs and good men, many of them now gone.

His foibles were confessed as well—his lust for bagels and his indecent devotion to air-conditioning and overstuffed chairs.

Along with the glory came the usual wounds we hunters and our dogs suffer, the puncturings by thorns and cuts from barbed-wire fences. Nothing major, though, until at age nine a torn knee ligament nearly ended his career. It was the injury every football running-back fears. He had the NFL surgery, without the insurance policy, and after a half year of patient rehabilitation he hunted on that rebuilt knee another three seasons.

English Foxhounds

Opposite: Golden Retriever

But I'd been reminded how quickly the clock was turning on our time together.

Though all the best images of him were locked away safely in memory, where negatives never get mislaid, I wanted more. I wanted a Rufus pup. He'd sired one litter when he was three. But I can tell you, in case you've never tried, it's no easy trick finding a bride for an elderly bird dog with a game leg.

I'd noticed women in our nearby park walking their Brittanys on leads, fine-looking prospects some of them—the dogs, I mean. But you can't rush up to lady strangers unannounced and say, "Let me tell you about something I have in mind . . ."

That likely would be misunderstood and might end up with you standing manacled in front of a judge.

Standard Poodles

Australian Shepherd

Finally, however, a match was made. In spring 1994, a fine litter of nine resulted, and I kept two: orange and white Pete (Rufus Repeater) and liver and white Holly's Bear. That autumn, a friend who hosts a syndicated outdoor show on television wanted to make a program featuring Rufus and his pups. During the filming on that December day, a quail fell on the skim ice of a frozen pond. Several dogs were working, but only old Rufus, at age 12, was willing to break ice 20 yards out to make the retrieve.

The next November, when the mornings sharpened, he waited at the door and would not be left behind. Sometimes, on uneven ground, he stumbled and fell. I pretended not to see. Cataracts had clouded the pupils of his amber eyes, but his nose told him all he cared to know. He found a bird, pointed it, and when it dropped he brought it to me. Neither of us knew it would be his last.

Then, as sooner or later happens to nearly everything we care most about, we lost him. It was shortly before Christmas 1995.

Irish Setters

One day he could not make his way onto his couch. The next evening he couldn't stand. All the skills of good veterinarians could not discover what had felled him. We kept him as long as it seemed reasonable to hope, then brought him from the clinic and I slept the last night with him on a pallet on the kitchen floor.

Our veterinarian friend, Dan, came to the house that Sunday morning. I'd saved a quail wing, a comfort for Rufus's journey. At the scent of it his ears came up, the dim eyes brightened. And in that moment I believe he remembered it all: the early risings, the car rides in darkness, fences he'd flown over on legs that never tired, the powerful smell of the covey before the rise. Just as he took the wing from my hand, we released him—let him go, not as some broken thing, but full of the passion that had ruled him.

Two months short of 13 years we'd had together. I counted up once, and of the 1,700-some columns of mine published during his lifetime, he'd made appearances in 50. That's not, I think, an unseemly number. There was one more to compose—the hardest one.

I buried him at the farm, wrapped in my hunting coat, in a

Labrador Retriever

favorite fence row of ours, facing a
thicket of wild plum where he and I
almost always had found a covey, and
marked the place with a pile of field
stones. Then, through hot tears, I
wrote a good-bye to him for the next
day's paper. It's one of the advantages
of personal journalism that you can
use it for personal purposes. What followed was astonishing.

Two news services sent out the column on their wires, and letters began
pouring in, hundreds of them, from
around the country. The newspaper
got more than 7,000 requests for reprints—nothing like it in the
editors' experience or mine. It wasn't until then that I understood how many friends he had. Some of them, most of them

Vizsla

perhaps, had never hunted. Others opposed hunting
fiercely. Some had never shared life with a dog of any kind.

But Rufus bridged those differences.

"Farewell, old friend," one reader wrote. "You have
granted us a lifetime of joy and wonder. You were our dog,
too." He was not just one man's companion, after all. In
some way, he'd belonged to all of them.

The editors proposed that I might write a book about
Rufus, but I wasn't sure I had the heart for it. I turned it in
mind from January until May, and decided finally that I
could do him better justice in a little book than I had in the
one column. So I did write it, and the paper published it as
a local book. And we supposed that was the end of it.

It wasn't. One of my daughters lives and works in New
York, and she had lunch with a friend one day who'd invited
a friend of his to join them. The friend's friend turned out to
be an editor with a publishing house, and my daughter men-

106

tioned the book to him. He borrowed it overnight, liked it, and passed it on.

To shorten the tale, the next spring it came out as a national book, then as an audio version, then in paperback. A reviewer for the *Baltimore Sun* wrote that Rufus had joined "such celebrated American canines as Gipson's Old Yeller, Jack London's Buck and Faulkner's Lion, Willie Morris' Skip and Truman Capote's

Standard Poodle

Queenie—all different but all revered, all now impervious to the savage onslaught of time, captured for posterity in black ink."

So he runs now in far fields, in parts of the country he never saw.

If I could trade the book for having Rufus back I'd do it in a minute. That being impossible, I take consolation from reading again, from time to time, some of those letters his friends wrote, in which they enclosed snapshots of their dogs and told of their own devotions and their griefs.

And there is another, even better consolation.

It will be October when you read this. The nights will have begun to cool, and the afternoons to shorten, as the planet tilts a fraction farther toward the dark. Soon, a frost will brush tan the crop fields and color the woodlots of my part of the midlands.

Through my window here I can see Pete and Bear, his sons, supervising the activity of squirrels in the walnut tree at the back of the yard. And with them there's a third, Bear's boy, Cyrus—a Rufus grandson. I am counting down the days to the season that bird dogs, and those of us who follow them, live for.

Rufus's temperament and his gift have passed intact to these generations that follow. In the flash of them across an autumn meadow, I will see him as joyous as he ever was, and young again.

—*October 2000, "Every Autumn, He'll Be at My Side"*

Opposite: Alaskan Malamutes

FOR
THE LOVE
OF DOGS

"Man's best friend," as it turns out, is an understatement.

Opposite: Samoyed

English Springer Spaniel

CHRIS WALKOWICZ

I remember the days when I used to come home from work, have
dinner, put my feet up and watch TV—now I rush home, let the
dogs out, pray I've beaten the old dog's bladder problems this
time, clean up after the dogs, water them, feed them, train them,
pat them, give pills, clean up the mess from the puppies, social-
ize pups, feed them, have a peanut butter and jelly sandwich,
clean up after the pups again, let the adults out again, and spend
the rest of the evening typing pedigrees, or reading an article on
"The Locomotion of Dogs Over the Age of Seven."

—*April 1988, "Having Fun"*

HILDE WEIHERMANN

The train heading for Denmark
on the way to Sweden and freedom that night in early May
1945, was composed of cattle
wagons, as had been all previous
ones used for transporting prisoners, but there was a difference; the cars were not packed
beyond capacity, there was room
enough for everyone to stretch
out on clean straw, and many
took the opportunity to sleep,
although one could not be certain whether the remarks of the
guards with respect to the destination could be believed.

Golden Retriever

Not only was Helga unable to sleep, she could not even relax,
a flaw that was to characterize her life always. Her thoughts
encompassed the past few years and, as she tried to catch a
glimpse of the scenery through the half-open door where the two

guards assigned to this car were positioned, in order to perhaps figure out the course of the journey, focused on an incident that had happened only about a week earlier, and whose outcome was responsible for her being now here on this train—it could have ended quite differently.

It was a cloudy morning that day late in April 1945, with the forebodings of impending doom in the air. One could sense from the behavior of the guards, from the way they looked, that the end of the war was not far away, and they well knew what was in store for them. The prisoners feared them now even more than before, afraid of their erratic actions and expecting the worst while still hoping to survive, particularly now that freedom was almost within reach.

The factory where the prisoners had worked in 12-hour shifts around the clock had recently been closed, as raw material had run out. Subsequently, there no longer was any work to be done. The large halls remained closed and silent.

Although it was the general consensus that without working it was possible to subsist longer on the almost nonexistent daily rations, Helga did not agree. She had volunteered to assist in the infirmary, as she had always felt that being occupied, no matter how hard and strenuous the task may be, was preferable to not doing anything; one had less time to brood and worry, at times almost forgot about being hungry. Helga was 22 years old, a small girl of slight build and quite inconspicuous, an advantage under the

Collie, 1930

Bulldog

circumstances. For almost three years she had been in camps now, in many different places, some as far as the Russian border, and since the fall of 1944 in this one near Hamburg.

During those last weeks of World War II the infirmary in particular was a place of terrible sadness, where despair reigned around the clock. The barrack was located close to the entrance of the camp, near the electric wire fence and the gate that separated the guards' quarters from those of the prisoners. When Helga looked through the fence, she would silently communicate with the German Shepherd Dog whose hut was just opposite the infirmary, several feet removed from the barbed wire. He was always on a leash, which had been fastened to his hut. It allowed him to move about

Labrador Retriever

in a small circle, just stopping short a few feet before the fence.

The Shepherd was a beautiful dog, a true representative of his breed, predominantly black with tan markings, straight ears on an impressive head, his face always reflecting alertness. In addition, he had at his disposal such a variety of facial expressions that sometimes, at least to the girl inside the camp, he seemed almost human. A very strong and powerful dog, his physique and movements conveyed this to even a distant observer, an animal that indeed seemed capable of performing all sorts of tasks that required intelligence as well as strength.

It was, of course, not possible to call the dog or convey any audible signs; the guards would have noticed and never tolerated that. The dog was not wholly attack-trained, but had been taught to detain anything that moved speedily, and the guards used to take him along when they marched the prisoners to and from the factory, just in case someone had the notion to try an escape under the cover of the blackout. However, since the work stoppage, the dog was almost always in or next to his hut.

Within a few days, despite the wire fence that always separated them, Helga considered the Shepherd, whose name she never learned, to be her friend. He seemed to wait for her to appear at the window of the barrack or outdoors in back of the infirmary. At times she would even dare to come a bit closer to the fence and silently motion to him to try a smile. He would then look straight at her, ears erect and tail waving, a picture of alertness. But somehow he instinctively seemed to perceive the risk of this communication, since, although his was a strong and typically Shepherd-like voice, he never barked or made a sound.

This friendship was perhaps one week old when Helga had to fetch something from the kitchen barrack, which was in close proximity to the infirmary. On the short way back to the sick barrack, she noticed the dog off his leash, just outside the closed gate, right across from where she walked. As usual, she waved to him, but failed to notice the guard who stood nearby and observed the scene. In a rage he screamed at her "I'll show you!" and then, while opening the gate, commanded the dog: "Get her!" Helga started to run toward the barrack, horrified and terribly scared, as she was well aware that the dog was trained to obey. But somehow it occurred to her, as she had seen attack-trained dogs before, that this one was different, did not look quite so frightening as those she had observed. It must have been these thoughts, running through her mind in split seconds, that made her stop and turn around to face the dog, who had stormed through the gate and was heading toward her.

As she looked directly at him, he caught her glance and almost instantly screeched to a halt, so abruptly that the tracks were visible on the ground. He was quite close—two to three more leaps and he would have caught her, but he now moved very slowly, whining and flattening his ears. When he reached her, he sat down in front of her, extending one of his paws and looking directly into her eyes, ears pinned back and tail waving. She took the paw into her hand, suddenly feeling quite calm, her fear subsiding.

The guard who had observed this strange encounter, as he stood in the open gate, expecting a quite different spectacle, was literally speechless for a few minutes, obviously unable to believe his own eyes. Finally, with an unusually shaky and not very forceful voice he ordered the dog to return to him: "You dumb dog, get out of there, you are even too stupid to know that you are supposed to go after these no-good prisoners. Instead you sit down and give her a paw, you fool. Back into your hut." Helga, hearing this, knew that the danger was over, but the dog had to leave. She put down his paw, mustered enough courage to touch his head ever so slightly and whisper: "Thanks and so long, good friend." He must have understood quite well, as he looked at her once more, turned around and headed for the gate. The guard closed it after him and mysteriously did not try to hit the dog, who quickly disappeared inside his hut. Helga headed back to the infirmary, knowing full well that this had been a very close call, whose outcome could have been the end for her. But the Shepherd was indeed her friend.

Smooth Fox Terrier, 1947

Boxer

Many years have passed since, a lot of things have happened, but no matter how important or crucial, whether good or bad, Helga always remembers the German Shepherd Dog who was instrumental in saving her life, the dog whose name she never knew.

—*March 1978, "A Friend in Need"*

MARION LANE

Shiu was a newcomer to our neighborhood and in two weeks had done the impossible: made friends with both my dogs. While Puff was usually happy to meet other dogs on our walks, The Wee, a Yorkie, had never met a dog she didn't hate.

Until Shiu.

Lin Shiu Yi was not an ordinary dog and certainly not an ordinary Pekingese. There wasn't a shred of Oriental reserve about him. He was friendly and happy to the point of plain silliness. To disarm a new acquaintance he would race through the repertoire of goofy behaviors like a whirling red dervish. If the dance on hind legs didn't work, he'd try half a back somersault, fall to the ground and roll over twice. No? Then how about a quick bow, a sideways leap into the air, and a finale of stiff-legged hops. I don't know which of these got through to The Wee, but she genuinely liked to see him, growling only occasionally when he acted like a dog.

I hadn't been able to learn much about Shiu. His owners were a young Chinese couple who didn't speak English yet. I'd seen them once in the vet's office, where Shiu entertained the entire waiting room. They'd beamed proudly at all the attention paid their dog but said nothing.

Mrs. Lin usually walked the dog. When Shiu caught sight of us he'd go into the air with a yip and start frog-hopping on the end of his lead, his tiny owner in tow. "Thank you, hello," she would say in greeting. "Thank you."

This morning Shiu spotted my dogs the same time they spotted him. I saw him levitate off the sidewalk, just as I felt myself being dragged forward. Then I noticed something fluttering around his collar.

Both the Lins were with Shiu today. They were backlit by the brilliant morning sunshine, and I recognized them by their silhouettes and by Shiu's squeals of joy.

Very few of the Chinese in my neighborhood had dogs. I knew two families with Chows, one young man with a mixed breed, and the Lins with Shiu. I wondered about their breed choices: Did they purchase here in this foreign land the dogs that reminded them of home? Had these young people ever known a Chow or Pekingese in China?

When the Lins came up to me they stopped politely. Shiu was doing mad pirouettes, and all eyes were drawn to him. It was a few seconds before I realized that the gay flutter on his collar was a length of shiny black ribbon. In the same instant I noticed the black armbands on his owners.

Bull Terrier

I heard myself say, "Oh." I couldn't think of one more thing to say. The Lins looked at each other across the universe, and the only sound was Shiu Yi's happy panting.

—*July 1989, "The Dogs of China"*

Airedale and Greyhound, 1952

Have you ever felt badly, either because of illness or emotional upset, and have you collapsed in a chair somewhere and suddenly found a Shetland Sheepdog licking your hand or looking at you, wagging its tail, somehow aware that you are troubled? I have heard Sheltie owners talk about this kind of thing time after time. Some dog trainers will tell you it is imagined, that a dog is just a dog, but to those of us with Shelties, it is the Sheltie's sensitivity that touches us and that we recognize. Most dogs have an enormous capacity for affection but it seems to me that the Sheltie, who is an especially devoted dog and as a shepherd, is a dog more dependent on human concern than some other kinds of dogs, can be one of the best kinds of pets.

—*April 1967, "Shetland Sheepdogs"*

Saint Bernard, circa 1940

Labrador Retriever

WILLIAM LYON PHELPS

The first dog that ever became part of my household, Iowa Lad, was the finest dog I have ever seen. He was a thoroughbred Irish Setter, being a grandson of Elcho; but he was an outsize dog, the largest Irish Setter I have known. He died in 1899—nearly eleven years old—and is buried in a human cemetery, being superior in character and intelligence to nearly all the men and women who lie there.

I never knew him to seek a fight with any other dog, and I never knew him to refuse a fight when another dog attacked him bodily, for he paid no attention to oral insults, and he never was defeated. One illustration will suffice.

On a cold November day, he had accompanied me shooting. Dusk was coming on as we entered a small town. We made for the railway station, to take the train home. Dog and man were both very tired. Near the station a huge dog of another breed rushed Lad and bit him in the nose, also knocking him over with the force of his sudden and unexpected impact. Lad rose and gave that bully a terrific licking. The big fellow went off howling, and I think he was as amazed as he was hurt. A group of people crowded around

Saint Bernard

Lad and told me that the big bully had been the scourge of the village. He had killed many pet dogs, had bitten several people, and was the terror of the town. They could hardly believe their eyes when Lad finished him off with such speedy efficiency.

I think the reason Lad won all his fights was because he never had the least trace of fear, and the other dog knew it. Lad was like Gene Tunney, in the way he illustrated the difference between confidence and conceit. He had no conceit, which was why other dogs attacked him; but he had all the confidence in the world. Which was why they attacked him only once . . .

I procured a kind of grandnephew, Rufus the Second, whose full name was Rufus H. Phelps, the H. standing for his maiden name, Hubbard.

This is the dog which died so recently and had so remarkable a personality. He was fearless, loyal, intelligent, thoughtful, and an excellent hunting dog. He was known universally for his literary associations. He loved the library and an open fire. He adored men of letters.

I suppose no other dog has ever had such aristocratic literary companions. Rufus was actually stroked by Joseph Conrad. Caressed by Hugh Walpole. Petted by G. K. Chesterton. And kissed by John Galsworthy.

In 1928, when my wife asked Bernard Shaw to write his name in one of his books which she had bought and brought for him, he drew his fountain pen with exactly the same flourish with which Lohengrin, in the opera, draws his sword, and then asked her what day it was. She replied that it was a very important day in Irish history, July 12, but much more Irishly important for another reason—"It is the birthday of our Irish Setter, Rufus H. Phelps."

Then Mr. Shaw wrote his name in his beautiful handwriting, and under it he inscribed: "Rufus' birthday."

So although Mr. Shaw never had the honor of meeting Rufus, he came as near to it as was possible.

The death of a dog with so many friends of literary importance naturally was of news value to the world. Therefore, I was not at all

Labrador Retrievers

Bernese Mountain Dog

surprised to learn that my loss had been cabled abroad; in fact, the *New York Herald*, Paris edition, carried a special cable from New Haven which ran as follows:

"Rufus famous Setter dog, belonging to Professor William Lyon Phelps of Yale University, dies at the noted critic's summer home in Huron City, Michigan, to-day. Rufus was the favorite pet of the Yale campus, and assisted during his lifetime at many memorable scholastic and cultural events.

Professor Phelps, as president of Chi Delta Theta, a permanent organization of Yale undergraduates formed to perpetuate the art of punning, had dubbed Rufus "my Cur Delta Theta" because of that society and the New Haven dog license tag.

Rufus is being mourned by his many friends here.

No matter what I called him, my Setter was my Setter, and his place is indeed a hard one to fill.

—December 1931, *"William Lyon Phelps Tells of His Dog, Rufus H. Phelps"*

GEORGE BERGER

"Iron Mask," by Tempa Lautze, is the first-place winner of the AKC GAZETTE's 16th annual fiction contest. It is a story about a duck hunter and his two Flat-Coated Retrievers—a bright, full-of-beans rookie, and an aging, seasoned campaigner; a tale of undying love and unfailing loyalty. I can relate to it, at least in part. It's been years since there has been a puppy at our house, but living with an older dog is a very real part of our lives. Ben, our Labrador Retriever, will be 15 in July.

It seems that Ben "has the genes," as some say about both

Borzoi

English Springer Spaniel

people and dogs who appear youthful in spite of their years. He didn't start to show any real sign of age until well past his 12th birthday, and, at that, just a few white hairs on his soft, black muzzle. You'd hardly notice. Passersby were always amazed to learn that this athletic, tail-thumping fellow was well into senior citizenship.

Now, finally, inevitably, the depth of age has set in. There's enough white on the face that anyone knows at a glance: old dog. His hips and spine are so weakened that going up or down stairs is a battle of determination versus pain. His eyesight is poor, and we often find him staring, as though lost, into some murky distance. He acts confused. His hearing is nearly gone, and most importantly, so is his heart.

But, in defiance of decaying senses and physical inability, Ben continues to show enormous kindness and devotion. He still scootches his nose up under my hand when I'm doing the lonely business of writing, just to let me know he's nearby. He still gets anxious and plants himself next to their bed when anyone in our family is sick. He still warns us when there's smoke in the house, even from a blown-out candle. And if there was big trouble, if we needed help in a hurry, he'd find a way to get it. I know he would.

—*May 2002, "Publisher's Note"*

Opposite: Siberian Huskies

130

GERALD AND LORETTA HAUSMAN

Shetland Sheepdog

In the beginning, so the old tales tell, there was the Creator and there was the dog. Mankind, quite simply, had not yet been invented. We may imagine a fathomless universe, a spectral void, or we may sketch in our thoughts about the perfect Creator, but we don't have to reach far to come up with a vision of our most ancient companion, our steadfast friend, the dog. In these old tales, we see that even before we possessed dogs, dogs possessed us. In this inevitable relationship, then, the under-pinnings of the dog, not as man's best friend, but as God's best friend, become clear.

—*April 1998, "The Magic of Myth"*

DOROTHY KILGALLEN

Isn't it strange how animals—especially dogs—influence the lives of human beings? I don't know about you, but I'm daffy about dogs—and most New Yorkers must be, too, because there are more dogs per capita here than in any other city in the world.

An authority on children recently declared that if every child in the nation had a dog to love, and be loved by, there hardly would be a juvenile delinquency problem. New York's Finest must think so, too, because I've never seen a policeman who wasn't an awful pushover for any pup that wagged a tail at him—have you?

— *August 1945, "Pushover for Pups"*

CECIL G. TREW

A very ancient legend tells that after He had created animals, God made Man as His masterpiece. But Man did not come up to God's expectation and his behavior was such that God, in disgust, caused a great chasm to open in the ground between Man and the other beasts.

Among the beasts stood the dog, gazing wistfully across the slowly widening gulf, until, unable to bear it any longer, the dog took a mighty leap, and landed by Man's side, where he has remained, more faithful than any other living creature, ever since.

—*April 1941, "Dogs of the Ancients"*

ELIZABETH H. ANDERSON

When I reach my Heaven, I hope to be greeted by a long row of dog friends that have loved me well and given me years of understanding companionship. Looking back over my life, I can recite the names of various dog reigns as I can those of the English kings and queens. With the exception of a few brief interregnums, I have never been without a dog from the time I learned to walk, clutching the curls of a large French Poodle, until now, when I am ruled by 14 Cairns.

—*January 1933, "Win or Lose, It's a Great Game"*

Collie

133

Bulldog

CLARA L. DOBBS

Many people who see my beloved pets ask me: "What are they good for?" and it is difficult to answer such inquires by replying that my dogs are good for nothing but loving. To the dog lover, of course, one does not have to explain that the joy of owning dogs is in the love one gives them, and the love they give in return.

The beauty of line and color in my dogs is as satisfying as the melodies the musician evokes from the pianoforte, the harmonies the artist lays with his brush on his canvas or the sculptor fashions from marble or bronze.

"What is it good for?" It is a stupid question. What is beauty good for?

Something essential is lacking in any nature that does not find joy in some one or more of the manifold aspects of beauty. For many years now my Chihuahuas have helped to satisfy this hunger for the beautiful. From the first one I ever owned, down to the latest born of my present family, there has been a succession of canine individuals as distinct in beauty and lovableness as one may find in human beings. And unlike human beings, I have yet to find in my dogs any ingratitude. Always they repay in devoted affection the care and tenderness expended for their comfort and well-being.

—July 1927, "True Stories of Real Dogs"

FRED C. KELLY

Every time I look at my old dog Badger, I think what a man among men he might have been if nature had not had other plans for him and insisted on his being born a dog. On the other hand, if he had been born a woman, what a wonderful wife he might have been! The more I think about it, the more I'm inclined to believe that it is futile for anybody to expect to find as many commendable wifely qualities in a woman as are commonly to be

135

Labrador Retriever

seen in a good Airedale. Perhaps the reason we have such great love for dogs is that they possess so many of the qualities that we should like to see in all our friends, but often fail to find.

Nearly everybody knows wives who have one or more attributes that endear them to their husbands. Possibly there are even wives here and there who possess *all* the more sought-after conjugal qualities. But there are comparatively few women, just as there are equally few men, who can equal an Airedale, or for that matter any other good dog, in unswerving loyalty and devotion. A good dog loves his friends just for the fun of loving them, without expecting anything in return.

—*September 1924, "What a Man Badger Would Be!"*

ROGER ROSENBLATT

For someone as generally uncommunicative and emotionally undemonstrative as Hector is, he exercises a disproportionate power over our family's cultural life. A friend gave us a candle in the shape of Hector—a West Highland White Terrier—that has come to be known as Candlector. Someone else gave us a Westie-shaped salt and pepper shaker set, which is called Silverector. On our bed is a small pillow bearing a stitched representation of a Westie (we have not named that one). And, at the back gate of our house, standing short, elegant, and tail up, is a stone (we call it cement) version of a Westie, known as Cemector.

This is a lot of mythmaking, considering that Hector himself does not acknowledge any gesture of piety. (He trots past Cemector twice a day without a sniff of recognition.) And yet, oddly, he justifies his deification.

He came into the world nine years ago, a result of the union of Claire Niege de Brilliant, a dog whose royal bearing I can only imagine, and her disrespectable consort, Doc. Doc, whom I met at the breeder's kennel where we acquired Hector, was the spitting image of the old roué who used to appear on the covers of *Esquire* magazine. The breeder introduced him as a character whose life's activities revolved wholly around his machismo. Ten seconds after his introduction, Doc lived up to his reputation by wetting the rug, as his owner called out plaintively, and without effect, "No, Doc! No, Doc!"

We were determined for obvious reasons not to have Hector follow in his father's footsteps, especially since, as a puppy, he could be explosively vicious, or as dog experts say, "territorial." Unluckily for us, the territory that Hector claimed was the entire house, and before he was surgically deprived of the strongest fea-

English Setter

ture of his father's personality, he was more terror than terrier. Even after his operation, Hector was one rough little customer. That is, until the Night of Hector's Nuclear War.

That was the night I went downstairs for a snack and found that Hector had just thrown up. Failing to understand that this deposit was a potential snack of his, I reached down and attempted to clean it up, at which moment he decided to make a snack of my hand. By now, I'd had it with Hector's demonstrations of temper. I picked up the very large crate in which he lived at the time, and raised it above my head, like Samson with a pillar. Hector watched me with an admixture of curiosity and apprehension. Then I brought the crate down hard on the floor, quite close to him. It made a mighty impressive noise, by which Hector was mightily impressed. From that night to the present, he

and I get along just fine, as he, quite rightly, regards me as someone who is capable of anything.

For my part, I have come to regard Hector with affectionate devotion, in spite of the fact that he does very few things. Apart from his toilet functions, he eats, sleeps, sits (though not always upon request), stretches (in that classic Westie way that makes him look like he's preparing for a jog), shakes his coat into place, yawns, and listens.

He has little or no discernible sense of humor. I have told him the following jokes, I don't know how many times, without eliciting as much as a titter: Man goes to a psychiatrist, tells the doctor he's worried because he thinks that he's a dog. "How long have you thought this?" asks the doctor. Man says, "Since I was a puppy." And this one: Did you hear about the dyslexic atheist who believed in dog? I thought that the subject matter might appeal to him.

I must say that he is very hard to read, and I prefer him that way. I know that there are books that tell us how to interpret what a dog is thinking in various situations, but, in my opinion, they miss the whole point about dogs. The appeal of Hector to me—and, I believe, of all dogs to everyone—is irrational, pure mystery. It is not what Hector thinks that matters to me. It's what he is. Not for nothing has my family created all those symbolic representations of him, those lares and penates that signify our devotion. Hector is our household god. Though neither dyslexic nor an atheist, I believe in him. He is faithful, to be sure, but he is also an object of faith. The less I know about him, the deeper my reverence.

What are the characteristics of a god, after all? Hauteur? Hector has plenty of that. Friendly as he is most of the time, he frequently turns from me and strikes a snooty pose similar to that of the stone lions outside the New York Public Library. Willfullness? He has that in abundance as well. When we're out strolling together, he will suddenly stop on a dime and squat like the

President Johnson and Him (Beagle), 1965

sphinx. Authority? All he has to do is yip in a particular way, and I a) replenish his food; b) free him from some ridiculous predicament; c) open a door for him; or d) play "the biting game." This delightful-to-him game may be played by two participants for up to 10 hours. It consists of my sticking my hand in his open mouth, and his biting me, but very gently. Actually, I'm not sure about the 10 hours. He could probably keep up the biting game for weeks. Gods play in mysterious ways.

Japanese Chin

So enamored with this game is he that he will often continue to play long after I've quit. He will roll from side to side, mouth open, wolflike, drunk on himself, and lost in dog heaven.

Still, his principal godlike quality—the reason I believe in dog—lies in his total incomprehensibility. Everything he does mystifies me: why he "decides" to settle in one place or another; why he chooses this position or that. Does he sit up or lie like a miniature polar bear rug with his legs extending out? Does he stare out the window, or at the wall?

And with all this, he seems far more capable of understanding me, than do I, him. If, for example, I'm feeling low or melancholy, he will enter the room in which I am sitting, stop in his tracks, and inspect me with his searching, black-eyed gaze. In a minute or so, he will approach and sit at my side, so that I may pet him. The theory behind this gesture seems to be that if I turn my attention from my troubles to his welfare, I will be gladdened by the experience. It always works. In a few seconds, whatever has been bothering me has vanished in the act of affection that he has generated. Like the Ancient Mariner, I bless Hector unaware, and the albatross of the moment drops from my neck.

They say that the joy in having a dog lies in the fact that he loves you unjudgingly. But I think it is because you love him unjudgingly—without complaint, without expectation of reward. The thing about dogs, and gods, is that they make better people out of those who believe in them.

—*September 2001, "The Dyslexic Atheist Who Believed in Dog"*

BREENA CLARKE

The long-awaited screen door was installed recently. It completes the renovation of our kitchen. Laura, our chocolate Labrador Retriever, didn't understand the screen door at first. It blocked her from running in and out. She, not meaning harm, pawed two holes

Welsh Terrier and Airedale

Weimaraner

in the screen five minutes after the man who installed it had left. I spit verbal fire at her, forcing her to cower.

My voice shocked her, and it hurt her feelings. And it hurt me to see her look. Her brown eyes were like a blowtorch to melt ice cubes. They were full of "I didn't mean to; I didn't understand; I promise I'll never do it again; please don't stop loving me." I was forced to cool my chastisement.

Here was a living, breathing being who was afraid of my anger, who respected my authority and depended upon me for intelligent guidance, food, shelter, and medical care, and I thought to banish her to a holding cell in hell because of a couple of feet of metal screen. I felt bad, but I felt good. I was engaged. I was a mother again. I was wrestling with the hurlyburly of parenthood.

I lost my most important mothering assignment when my son, my only child, died in an accidental fall 12 years ago at the age of 14. Recovering from the shock and pain of this grief is complex. You've trained for a role you're no longer required to fill. It was a role I cherished. What do you do with all those motherhood muscles? Is your heart too encumbered by sadness to take on loving another young human? My dog daughters, Hannah and Laura, have agreed to be cared for and cared about by me and my husband. They're keeping us human while we recover ourselves. They're helping us with the pain. We got Hannah, our black Lab, several years after our son died. I won't be specific as to exactly when because I'm afraid to count her years. She came when she was eight weeks old. I took a week's vacation to get her settled in. I spoiled her in the time-honored fashion of Southern mothers. I fed her— scrambled eggs with ground beef, cheese, and rice. I loved cooking for her. Before long she had become a furry, black barrel. When I went on a business trip, my husband weaned her to dog food.

The thing these dogs can't replace is the child's function as arrow into the future. They don't look forward and most likely will not outlive us. This is a powerful check on the human tendency to always be planning for tomorrow. These dogs look us in the eyes and say, "Today. Today. Just today."

Little by little my husband and I have stopped mourning for the past and stopped mourning for the future that won't pan out.

—September 2001, "Dog Daughters"

BOYD WRIGHT

Time has snuck up on me. About halfway through this past year, I turned 67; a month later my Golden Retriever, Sky, turned nine. Recently, by the traditional rule of thumb of seven dog years to each human year, our ages converged. Now he's the older one. This has been quite a jolt.

This sudden switch in our ages has hit me hard. We don't have anything like this in human relationships. We move along through the years with the same comfortable age span separating us. Today, my wife is exactly as many years younger as I am as the day we were married. My children have progressed from infancy to parenthood (and I to grandparenthood), but the differences in our ages have remained the same. Time plays no favorites with us; the rhythm of life moves on at a steady pace.

But with our beloved pets, time does play tricks. It allows no stable buffer of years between us.

German Shepherd Dog

143

Instead, time marches to a meaner drum, crunching years without mercy. While we move along at human speed, our dogs fast-forward into old age.

—January 1996, "Time and My Dog"

ARTHUR FREDERICK JONES

There is nothing more interesting—nor more refreshing—than a whole kennel of good dogs. They represent life in its finest expression. Growing and developing continually, their personalities provide a definite elixir that acts as a stimulant to the human being.

—March 1933, "Cosalta Raises Friendly Dogs"

W. LIVINGSTON LARNED

There, across from me, tonight, as I tap these words off on a machine, is a dog.

A moment ago, he came up to me, rubbed his shaggy head against my knee and words were unnecessary. He was saying, as best he could:

"I love you. You are my master. All I ask is your kindly notice. You came in, this evening, with never a word for me. Yet, all day long, I had waited for just that. I knew the hour of your homecoming. I knew when your step would sound on the walk outside. I had not seen you since morning. I wanted you to express pleasure over seeing me; me, a friend, indeed."

And, after a pause:

"I had expected you to make a fuss over me; you, of all others. It has seemed an eternity since you left this morning. The moment I heard your step, I scratched at the door and whined to be left out. I wanted you to know that I was happy to see you. And in you came and paid no attention to me. Oh, dear master, dogs have

144

hearts. Only a kindly pat on the head would have sufficed."

And there he was, stretched out on a rug, looking at me, with wistful, hurt eyes. I had been remiss. I had neglected one of the few real friends in my treasure chest of life. He would keep his distance until I displayed some sign of the old affection.

I called him over. Reluctantly he came, one laggard foot following the other. He could not be sure, as yet, that I meant all that my manner suggested. Edging up, he thrust a rugged paw upward and into my hand. Then his shaggy head swayed downward until it pressed against my knee.

There was more real, true friendship in this than I have found in a majority of supposed "friends." He wanted to be loved. Mind you, that is the deepest and most profound expression of friendship and loyalty. You must like the person that you would have love you. It is humiliating to have to plead for love. Only its open and unqualified expression, without urge or intent, is worth a hang.

And, having received a pat on the head and a look of regard, he was content to wander quietly back to his corner of the rug and to lie there, those eager eyes turned in my direction.

It is certain in my mind that had sudden danger menaced me, had a ruffian entered the house and attacked me, this dog would have freely risked or sacrificed his life in my behalf. And all he asked, in return, was a bit of love.

—*August 1927, "My Dog, Who Is Faithful Ever"*

Bloodhound

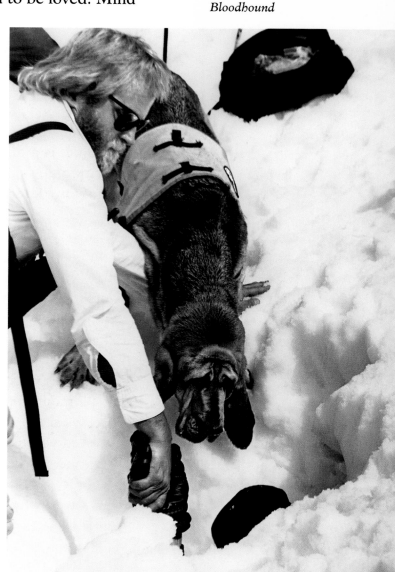

145

CONTRIBUTORS

Rick Bass is the author of 18 books of fiction and nonfiction, including *Colter: The True Story of the Best Dog I Ever Had*. He lives in northwest Montana with his family, where he is active in a variety of conservation activities.

George Berger is the publisher of AKC magazines.

Anne Elizabeth Blochin is the author of the books *So You're Going to Get a Dog?* and *That Dog of Yours*.

Bud Boccone has been an editor and writer for AKC Publications since 1998. For 10 years previously he wrote and illustrated stories for *Baseball America* magazine. He is a two-time recipient of the Manhattan Association of Cabaret's MAC Award for excellence in comedy writing and directing.

Phoebe Booth began in purebred dogs in 1965 and has been breeding Whippets since 1972. She is an exhibitor, handler, dog-show photographer, and currently the AKC GAZETTE breed columnist for Whippets. Her dogs compete in all areas of the sport.

Breena Clarke is the author of the novel *River, Cross My Heart*. She lives with her husband and their dogs in New Jersey.

Francis V. Crane and his wife, Mary, imported from France in 1931 the first Great Pyrenees dogs in the United States. They also established the first kennel and breeding program for this breed at their home in Massachusetts.

C. W. Gusewelle has written for the *Kansas City Star* since 1955. Besides his newspaper reporting and commentary, his articles and short fiction have appeared in *Harper's*, *American Heritage*, and *The Paris Review*. In

1997 he wrote and narrated the Kansas City documentary *This Place Called Home*, which was awarded a regional Emmy. His latest documentary, *Water and Fire: A Story of the Ozarks*, was judged best documentary and Best in Show in a competition among more than 70 public television stations in the United States.

Gerald and Loretta Hausman are the authors of *The Mythology of Dogs, The Mythology of Cats,* and *The Mythology of Horses.* They have also written *Dogs of Myth* and *Cats of Myth* for younger readers, as well as *The Metaphysical Cat.* The Hausmans live in Bokeelia, Florida, with two Great Danes, a Dachshund, two cats, and a parrot.

Lori Herbel is a freelance writer and photographer, and her work has appeared in many magazines and books, including *Ranch Dog Trainer, Dogs in Review, The Complete Australian Cattle Dog,* and *Kids Plus Dogs Equals Fun.*

Arthur Frederick Jones was an editor and writer for the GAZETTE for more than 30 years. His books include *Care and Training of Dogs, The Treasury of Dogs,* and *The World Encyclopedia of Dogs.*

Fred C. Kelly was an author, newspaperman, and columnist. He wrote *The Wright Brothers*—the only authorized biography of the famous inventors.

Dorothy Kilgallen was a renowned journalist during the Kennedy era, as well as a TV personality, serving many years as a panelist on the game show *What's My Line?*

Marion Lane is a former executive editor of the AKC GAZETTE and the current editor of *ASPCA Animal Watch.* Among her numerous publications on pet training and health care are the books *The Humane Society of the United States Complete Guide to Dog Care* and *You and Your Puppy.*

W. Livingston Larned wrote articles and poetry for several magazines, his most famous poem being perhaps "Father Forgets." He was also the author of the book *Illustration in Advertising.*

Freeman Lloyd was an avid sportsman and writer. He contributed frequently to the AKC GAZETTE, writing articles about numerous breeds, and was considered an expert on famous British dogs. He also wrote articles for *National Geographic* and was the author of the book *All Spaniels.*

Doug Marlette, born in Greensboro, North Carolina, began drawing political cartoons for the *Charlotte Observer* in 1972. He joined the *Atlanta Journal-Constitution* in 1987, *New York Newsday* in 1989, and the *Tallahassee Democrat* in 2002. His editorial cartoons and his comic strip,

Kudzu, are syndicated in hundreds of newspapers worldwide. He has won every major award for editorial cartooning, including the 1988 Pulitzer Prize.

Robert Olmstead is the author of the novels *America By Land, A Trail of Heart's Blood Wherever We Go,* and *Soft Water,* as well as a collection of short stories, *River Dogs* and a memoir, *Stay Here With Me.*

Padgett Powell has published four novels and two story collections. His novel, *Edisto,* was a nominee for the National Book Award. His fiction has appeared in *The New Yorker, Harper's, Esquire, Paris Review,* and in the anthologies *Best American Short Stories, O. Henry Prize Stories,* and *New Stories from the South.* His nonfiction and reviews have appeared in *The New York Times Book Review, Georgia Review, Oxford American, Harper's,* and *Best American Sportswriting.* He is a professor of English at the University of Florida.

William Lyon Phelps was a distinguished professor of English at Yale University, as well as a literary critic, lecturer, and prolific writer.

Roger Rosenblatt is the author, most recently, of *Anything Can Happen: Notes on My Inadequate Life and Yours.*

Braxton B. Sawyer was a breeder of American Foxhounds and wrote many pieces on the history and state of dog shows.

Richard Schickel is the author of over thirty books, including *Good Morning, Mr. Zip Zip Zip,* and *Woody Allen: A Life in Film,* both published in 2003. He has also produced, written, and directed over 30 television documentaries, most recently *Charlie: The Life and Art of Charles Chaplin,* a feature documentary for Warner Brothers. Richard Schickel reviews movies for *Time* and writes a monthly column for *The Los Angeles Times Book Review.*

Jane Smiley is the author of ten novels, the mother of three children, and the owner of twelve horses and three dogs. She lives in California.

Albert Payson Terhune (1872–1942) was the author of over twenty-two books about dogs, including the *Lad, A Dog* series and *Gray Dawn.* A Collie enthusiast, Terhune founded the famous Sunnybank Kennel in Wayne County, New Jersey.

Cecil G. Trew was the author and illustrator of over a dozen books on wildlife and animals, particularly horses and dogs.

Chris Walkowicz is an AKC judge who has published more than eight hundred articles and columns in major canine publications. She has also authored or coauthored eight books, including *Successful Dog Breeding: The Complete Handbook of Canine Midwifery,* and *The Perfect Match: A Dog Buyer's Guide,* She is president of the Dog Writers Association of America.

Hilde Weihermann was born in Frankfurt am Main, Germany. Having just completed her fortieth year as an employee of the AKC, much of her life has been spent for and with dogs. She is an avid photographer, and in addition to her written contributions, several of her images of dogs have appeared in the AKC GAZETTE.

Leon F. Whitney was a well-respected veterinarian and a pioneer geneticist. He wrote many books on pet care, including *The Complete Book of Dog Care,* and on animal genetics, including *How to Breed Dogs.*

Boyd Wright is a retired newspaper editor who has written widely for national magazines. His books include *I Want to Believe, But . . . A Navigator for Doubters, Bay the Moon,* and *Jockey Hollow.* He lives in Mendham, New Jersey, with his wife, Jean, and their rescued Greyhound, Jamie.

Other Contributors:

Elizabeth H. Anderson
John Billings Jr.
Col. W. F. S. Casson, D. S. O.
Clara L. Dobbs
Charles Forrest Dowe
David S. Edgar Jr.
Sarah M. Greenhow
Robert Hanks
Jeri Holloway
John Kemps
W. Ruloff Kip
E. J. Lewis
Otus Renard
Wallace Reyburn
Louise Sprague
Marian F. Wolcott

PHOTO CREDITS

archives; 70: Freudy photo, courtesy Dalmatian Club of America; 71: AKC photo archives, photo by Percy Jones; 73: AKC photo archives, Quaker Oats; 74: © Veite-Wauhop; 77: © AKC, photo by Mary Bloom; 78: © Diane Lewis; 80: © Eric Albrecht; 81: © Tien Tran Photography; 82: © Diane Lewis; 83: © Joseph C. Leo; 84: AKC photo archives; 85: © Shot on Site Photography; 86: © Diane Lewis 87: AKC photo archives; 88: © Tien Tran Photography; 89: © Tara Darling; 90: © Beth Hanson; 91: © AKC, photo by Tara Darling; 92: © Diane Lewis; 93: © Diane Lewis; 94: © Janis Watts; 95: © Hustace Photography; 96: © Chet Jezierski © AKC; 97: © Kim MacDonald; 98: © Bonnie Nance; 99: © Steve Surfman; 100: © AKC, photo by A.H. Rowan; 101: © Dwight Dyke; 102: AKC photo archives; 103: © Diane Lewis; 104: AKC photo archives, photo by W.M. Brown; 105: © Hustace Photography; 106: (top) © AKC, photo by Chet Jezierski; (bottom) © Hustace Photography; 107: AKC photo archives, © Paula Wright; 108: © Kent and Donna Dannen; 110: © Kent and Donna Dannen; 112: © Bonnie Nance; 113: © Mary Thrasher; 114: AKC photo archives; 115: © Mary Bloom; 116: © Renee Esordi; 119: AKC photo archives, courtesy Lawrence McNally; 120: © Karen Overy; 121: © Connie Whitmer; 122: AKC photo archives; 123: AKC photo archives; 124: © Close Encounters of the Furry Kind, LLC; 125: © Caroline Wills; 127: © Hustace Photography; 128: © Bernd Guenter; 129: © Bonnie Nance; 130: © Carol Little; 131: © Warren Boyer, courtesy Joy Graeme Messinger; 132: © Ed Scheff; 133: © Tammy Russell-Rice; 134: © Arlene Siegal; 136: © AKC, photo by Mary Bloom; 137: © Diane Cornell; 139: AKC photo archives; 140: courtesy Betty Stovall; 141: AKC photo archives; 142: © Jeff Zucker; 143: © Karen Lessig; 145: © Randall Howell; 146: © Denver Bryan/www.denverbryan.com.

Back jacket photograph credits (left to right):

Akita, © Close Encounters of the Furry Kind, LLC; Weimaraners, © Harry Giglio; Polish Lowland Sheepdog, © Mary Bloom; Maltese, © Alice Su; Schipperke, © Alice Su; Labrador Retriever, © Denver Bryan/www.denverbryan .com; Great Danes, © Mike Johnson.